Bible Word Search
New Testament

by
Christine R. Jackson

illustrated by Shelly Rasche

Cover by Dan Grossmann

Shining Star Publications, Copyright © 1993

ISBN No. 0-86653-765-1

Standardized Subject Code TA ac

Printing No. 9876543

Shining Star Publications
1204 Buchanan St., Box 299
Carthage, IL 62321-0299

Unless otherwise indicated, the New International Version of the Bible was used in preparing the activities in this book.

Dedication

To my patient mother, who will never get the credit she deserves for all that she's done (Ecclesiastes 3:1-8), and to my father, who was willing to be the guinea pig who field tested these puzzles (Philippians 4:13).

Thanks to you both.
I love you very much!

Christine

Table of Contents

To the Teacher/Parent

Bible Word Search—New Testament is comprised of thirty-nine word searches from well-known stories in the New Testament. This book will help make the stories come "alive" as you search the Scriptures, in groups or individually. Most word searches have bonus activities that reveal hidden objects or verses from the leftover letters.

Each word search has a Scripture reference from which the words in the word bank are taken. Some words are found more than once. A number in parentheses beside the word indicates the number of times the word appears in the puzzle. However, if a word is found within another circled word it is not to be counted. If a word has been shortened from the original Scripture, it is also in parentheses. Words may not overlap by more than two letters.

May this book challenge you to look into the Scriptures and find more about the stories of the New Testament.

There is an answer key to refer to, as a last resort.

Enjoy!

The Birth of Jesus
Matthew 2:1-12

Read the Scripture, then circle each word from the word bank hidden in the puzzle. Words may appear forward or backwards, moving up, down, or diagonally.

```
O K E L A P R O Q C T L O V E D J O D A C K E D L
O J L G M N K P A E S S V W P E R M R N R D D J B
P C N F I D V V A R I T E A T K O V T K M O E T S
L M H L T K T I M B T A R S D M R H L R J R D E P
P T U E S G C Q O H H R J E N F J F I E O H G F N
R Q R S T M S J D D E W O B A I T S T D I S L M R
S G S J P I H K K T H E Y D L S I D S N J G K Q O
W I P L U V T N K X B X E R T S U U Q R S C T U R
O H X W O R S H I P Y E D A S H P R O P H E T H E
M N R O B T U B N I J E T E A E T U E D A E H A C
L Q B R S T F I G T S E M H E P N L D I A S U W B
T P N Q Y M I H O T H R S O L H E E A S T U W J W
S D K E K M Y X F M S E A U C E S R M E Y K I L M
V R H U T L N M T I M E I E S R H S U R T S U S N
G L V S R F I A H H D A I R L D E E D M W P D R U
S S I C T S P R E U T S E R S X R P M O P R T D I
O M J U U W D Y J J O P U M P E D E O Q M H L P T
K D G J M L R A E L O D I R I F A E A R O M M J I
B L F C O T F R W A Q D K D L N E R N M T L J O M
A C B G N T U O S W U S G T N S C I C R E B M H K
K B O U E S N U A R T E H L M C U E H H A O K S B
S G O R A E X T W T R U L U N F B S N C C W D P E
T C D L I H C E S R T Q U K S N S Y E S H E E L C
I X E D N I F R U K M N T D W C I E W J E D K A T
T M A G I S E T S R I K G F E V P O B A R O S C G
F E K A M B V U K E D G S B R U I P E R S F A E A
```

Word Bank

EAST	INCENSE	ONE (2)	TEACHERS	BUT	FIND	ME (9)
BETHLEHEM	MYRRH	TO (6)	ASKED	OVERJOYED	MY (3)	AFTER
LEAST	BORN	WAS	ON	STAR	JESUS (2)	THEY
PROPHET	OF (2)	WORSHIP	GO (3)	MAGI	TIME	JUDEA
LAND	COME	TREASURE(S)	AS (6)	SHEPHERD	AHEAD	DREAM
THE (2)	THEIR	WARNED	TOO	CHILD	MAKE	SAW (2)
SEARCH	HEARD	HIM (2)	ROUTE	HIS (2)	MARY	SENT
JERUSALEM	SAID	RULERS	COUNTRY	GIFTS	LAW	ISRAEL
KING OF THE JEWS	PLACE	BOWED (2)	GOLD	BY (3)	REPORT	
CHIEF PRIEST(S)						

Bonus: To discover what the wise men followed, shade in the circled words and the *X*'s.

SS2880

The Beatitudes

Matthew 5:1-12

Read the Scripture, then circle each word from the word bank hidden in the puzzle. Words may appear forward or backwards, moving up, down, or diagonally.

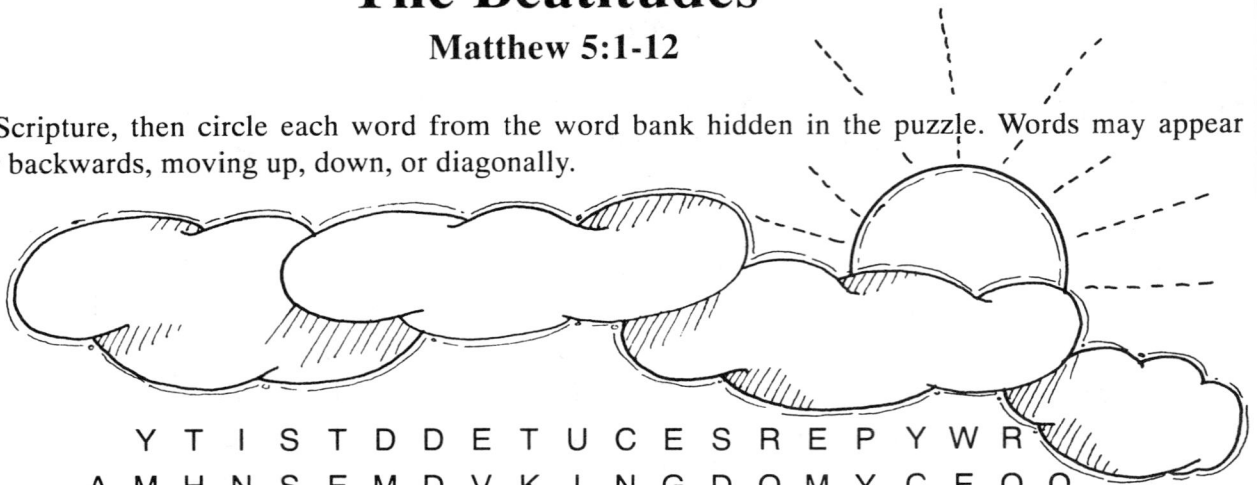

```
      Y T I S T D D E T U C E S R E P Y W R
      A M H N S E M D V K I N G D O M Y C E O O
      S M I E R S E I D I S C I P L E S E R N F D O
    N S E H I S E S F I L L E D P R O P H E T S E H P
  L E D H H E K N R B M U N G M Z E W I T M D T T E E S
  U V W T L T I S C R D W S E M Z J A R R A O S R S A R
  F A O B E A N U Y U O S A T O L C M I E C W D O A C I
  I E R A T W H O M D R D O G P S E T T G E N W F W E E
  C H C N O H E E M A E V E T T S M S X N R U O M E M H
  R H U H E E R T Z P D O R F E D A L G U U F R O M A T
  E O S B R N I H V E S B P U R E A R T H P O C C A K H
  M G R E A T T G A R N F R D D W O N H E A V E N C E E
  B H U N G E R I T U T J M L L O N G I E C I O J E R Y
    E D R A W E R S T U S O N E L W C R B E F O R E S
    G N A G E B C E O E E S O P N T S P E O P L E
      A D A L G P I M A K R S E T U T L U S N I
      N A L L T P Y W H O N P T K E S L A F
      W E R E U O Y B L E S S E D N I K
```

Word Bank

CROWDS (2)	POOR	MOURN	MERCY	GLAD (2)	SAW
SEE (3)	SPIRIT	COMFORTED	HEART	REWARD	OF (6)
ALL	KINGDOM	MEEK	NOW	IN (4)	THEIRS
MOUNTAINSIDE	HEAVEN (2)	INHERIT	GOD	HIM	BEFORE
SAT	EARTH	PURE (2)	PROPHETS	FOR	SHOWN
GREAT	HUNGER (2)	SON(S)	FILLED	DOWN	THIRST (2)
PEOPLE	THEY (2)	WHEN	DISCIPLES	ARE (2)	KIND(S)
RIGHTEOUSNESS	INSULT	WENT	BE (6)	CAME (2)	SAY
PERSECUTED	FALSE(LY)	HE (16)	TEACH	THEM	MERCIFUL
EVIL	BEGAN (2)	BLESSED (2)	THE (2)	REJOICE	WERE
PEACEMAKERS	IS (6)	YOU			

Bonus: Shade in the area that has no circled words and find the secret letter. This letter is a clue to the word Jesus spoke nine times in this sermon. (One *X* is not used.)

Prayer
Matthew 6:5-15

Read the Scripture, then circle each word from the word bank hidden in the puzzle. Words may appear forward or backwards, moving up, down, or diagonally.

```
E  V  O  L  T  M  E  N  H  E  V  I  G  R  O  F  I  S  P  T
V  I  N  E  E  S  N  U  S  H  K  I  N  G  D  O  M  R  S  E
I  S  E  T  I  R  C  O  P  Y  H  O  W  E  Y  O  A  U  R  R
L  S  S  H  E  O  O  E  U  N  L  D  W  P  S  Y  R  E  E  C
E  E  T  N  A  M  E  O  O  A  R  O  O  D  A  O  H  Y  N  E
K  U  E  A  O  K  P  T  M  M  L  U  B  R  F  T  L  A  R  S
I  G  E  T  N  H  E  T  R  L  S  N  A  G  A  P  I  C  O  T
L  O  R  K  N  D  R  H  A  E  A  V  B  F  U  O  Y  E  C  B
D  G  T  N  N  U  I  H  H  T  S  A  B  E  C  A  U  S  E  E
R  A  S  I  T  L  L  N  E  O  I  W  L  E  D  B  R  E  A  D
A  N  K  H  B  E  Y  L  G  O  N  O  I  S  D  R  O  W  R  M
E  Y  S  T  U  R  L  N  N  E  E  D  N  E  V  A  E  H  T  I
H  S  A  R  E  C  E  I  V  E  D  A  G  M  E  R  U  O  H  H
```

Word Bank (words in bold)

"And when **you pray**, do not be **like** the **hypocrites**, for they **love** to pray **standing** in the **synagogues** and on the **street corners** to be seen by **men**. I **tell** you the **truth**, they have **received** their reward in full. But when you pray, go into your **room**, **close** the **door** and pray to your **Father**, **who** is **unseen**. Then your Father, who sees what is done in **secret**, will reward you. And when you pray, do not **keep** on **babbling** like **pagans**, for they **think** they will be **heard because** of their **many words**. Do not be like them, for your Father knows what you **need** before you **ask him**. This, then, is how you should pray: 'Our Father in **heaven**, **hallowed** be your **name**, your **kingdom** come, your will be done on **earth** as it is in heaven. Give us today our daily **bread**. **Forgive** us our **debts**, as we also have forgiven **our** debtors. And lead us not into **temptation**, but deliver us from the **evil** one.' For if you forgive men when they **sin** against you, your heavenly Father will also forgive you. But if you do **not** forgive men their sins, your Father will not forgive your sins."   Matthew 6:5-15

Bonus: To discover the beginning of the Lord's Prayer, write below the uncircled letters in the puzzle.

_____

Jesus Sends Out the Twelve
Matthew 10:1-10

Read the Scripture, then circle each word from the word bank hidden in the puzzle. Words may appear forward or backwards, moving up, down, or diagonally.

```
B K I P T Q L P E L I E E S K R J B G A U P B P M T N
C E A M B E S N A E L C O C N N O T E V I E C E R E M
A D E K O L E A R S I M S W E T W E A R E J N O J E K
H L P D I S C I P L E A M N V U H N D N A A O N U L I
I J O S I C K J O H N T A V A N O T H I M M M S D B R
L T G N O L A A I S S T B U E I O E U B L E I E A A G
P O H E A L T M L S I H V G H C F R B T K S S L S U W
E K L W D V S E I H M E M L W D F N T O M S D I I B O
G M R E T A B S V E O W I R G K T F E S M O A T S V P
U S E F W C J S E E N R M Q F A H R T V X N E N C D F
M Z E V P O U O E P P O O U S Y I W K C U O D E A Y A
T U P D E M P N B N E T L B X R J B S O L F E G R Y S
A P M U P C E O A S T C P C P D C X W P J A H D I W E
S E I Z T F L F R A E E K Z B E T C F I H L T E O X T
A M B B B S J Z T M R L A P K P T N J L I P E L T P R
M T K P V R C E H O T L S G U K A V A G W H S L I L E
E P A S F X E B O H H O R Y B F C I G E A A I A N K O
K A S E J C T E L T A C B A M D L H R R T E A C A P P
R B R O M N D D O P D X P S R Q J K D U V U R N M L U
U O Z B E E C E M I D A Y Q W X T R T L N S D M C H L
K M J F K G X E E L A T M K C P P U E O I R S R U X Q
H T W L P E M T W I E O U A A W B W T H E L P D M O M
A M U E I U Z H O H U N P W T G T U O W S R Q Y A E Z
S V L L G H P E F P S O T B M I S A N D A L S O D N D
R T S N P N C D R I V E E M C V N A T I R A M A S L H
P V L M G Q F S T A F F S V Z E M E S S A G E E H D K
K C M H R K B A R T X E T G A S L O S T N O M E D L L
M R H B T A I H M A M N L B F M U V R P E M S Y T G I
```

Word Bank

ANDREW, SIMON PETER, JAMES SON OF ZEBEDEE, JOHN, PHILIP, BARTHOLOMEW, THOMAS, MATTHEW, JAMES SON OF ALPHAEUS, DISCIPLE, THADDAEUS, SIMON, TWELVE, GENTILES, JUDAS ISCARIOT, SAMARITAN(S), HEAL, CLEANSE, DRIVE, RECEIVE, RAISE THE DEAD, GIVES, EVIL, SICK, GO (3), LOST, SHEEP, ISRAEL, MESSAGE, DEMON(S), SANDALS, ENTER, TUNIC, HEAVEN, HIM (2), DO (8), OF (2), OUT, WHO (2), AND, HE (10), THE (2), IN (6), IS (16), NO (8), TAX COLLECTOR, EXTRA, STAFF, ARE (2), NOT (5), ALONG, HIS (2), ALONG, CALLED, SENT

Bonus: Shade in the circled words to find how many disciples Jesus had.(Two *X*'s are not used .)

Jesus Walks on the Water
Matthew 14:22-36

Read the Scripture, then circle each word from the word bank hidden in the puzzle. Words may appear forward or backwards, moving up, down, or diagonally.

```
D  C  D  I  M  M  E  D  I  A  T  E  L  Y  S
E  A  A  D  E  I  D  D  W  O  R  C  L  A  E
S  U  E  D  N  A  H  I  A  J  U  E  A  R  N
S  G  H  D  S  F  N  S  V  U  L  S  N  P  T
O  H  A  U  O  D  R  A  E  F  Y  W  D  A  O
R  T  S  U  N  U  L  K  S  S  N  E  M  O  U
C  E  R  Y  O  S  B  O  A  T  S  E  M  O  C
J  T  N  R  F  I  T  T  H  S  S  L  L  I  H
H  G  C  T  G  N  E  D  I  S  T  A  N  C  E
B  N  L  N  O  K  E  M  D  E  L  A  E  H  D
E  I  I  U  D  I  S  C  I  P  L  E  S  W  K
G  N  M  O  R  I  L  A  T  H  C  T  A  W  A
G  E  B  C  D  O  E  L  P  O  E  P  V  E  O
E  V  E  R  R  D  E  I  F  I  R  R  E  T  L
D  E  D  D  D  R  O  W  E  G  A  R  U  O  C
```

Word Bank

IMMEDIATELY	DISTANCE	COURAGE	TRULY	HEALED	JESUS
LAND	COME	SON OF GOD	DIED	DISCIPLES	WAVES
CROSSED	MEN (2)	CLOAK	BOAT	WIND	SINK
SENT	CLIMBED	AHEAD	FOURTH	LORD	WORD
EVENING	DISMISSED	WATCH	SAVE	COUNTRY	PRAY
CROWD	TERRIFIED	HAND	PEOPLE	FEAR	HILLS
CRIED	CAUGHT	BEGGED	DOUBT	TOUCHED	

Bonus: To discover the theme of this story, write the uncircled letters on the lines below.

_____

_____

Shining Star Publications, Copyright © 1993

SS2880

The Transfiguration
Matthew 17:1-13

Read the Scripture, then circle each word from the word bank hidden in the puzzle. Words may appear forward or backwards, moving up, down, or diagonally.

```
D O N J A M E S T B E R E H T P L E
I S R E H C A E T D E S O N L L N W
A N F R A R E S T O R E D E E O I H
W I S H D W H O E W E E A T H N A O
N I A T N U O M L N H S M S T J D M
E T H E R D U O L C E A Y I I E S B
U V H E R U S L U D N A L L A S E R
O O O R R E C O G N I Z E D O U H O
W A Y L E K T T E D D E N E E S T T
D E P O L E V N E D E N H I G H O H
I U R E F F U S P D I O O L D T L E
S H E M A S I H T Y F L J N L I C R
C X I S F A F T E R I O U S G E E A
I H A L R E A D Y L R O W H N T F E
P O K S A O C N A E R K T E L I D M
L X U C I E E W P G E E D E L H I O
E N T J D B R I G H T D H E S W A C
S U V O I C E T H E M S E L V E S S
```

Word Bank

SIX	WHITE	FELL	THERE	MOSES	GROUND
JAMES	ELIJAH	TERRIFIED	JOHN	WISH	TOUCHED
BROTHER	THREE	AFRAID	LOOKED	HIGH	SHELTER(S)
DOWN	BRIGHT	INSTRUCTED	TELL (2)	TEACHERS	LAW
MOUNTAIN	CLOUD	RAISED	RESTORE	THEMSELVES	ALREADY
ENVELOPED	FACE	COME	RECOGNIZE	HIM	SON
SHONE	LOVE	VOICE	MAN	SUFFER	SUN (2)
LISTEN	PLEASED	CLOTHES	DISCIPLES	JESUS	AFTER
LED	LIGHT	SAID	SEEN	WAY	DEAD
ALL (2)	THIS	WHOM	ASK(ED)	SURE	
ONE	YOU				

Bonus: To discover what Jesus' disciples heard and saw, write the uncircled letters on the lines below.

_____

_____

The Lord's Supper

Matthew 26:17-30

Read the Scripture, then circle each word from the word bank hidden in the puzzle. Words may be written forward or backwards, moving up, down, or diagonally.

```
O  G  E  T  I  K  L  F  A  E  B  N  C  R  E  U  H  T  G  P  W
K  I  C  E  N  M  Y  H  E  L  B  A  T  T  F  E  A  S  T  F  C
A  Y  E  L  E  T  A  R  B  E  L  E  C  N  J  D  H  D  E  G  E
V  I  R  P  N  T  E  L  L  W  O  B  U  A  E  N  T  E  A  B  W
Y  E  T  I  I  B  T  M  E  H  O  G  P  N  S  R  U  P  C  O  N
J  O  A  C  L  L  S  E  L  O  D  A  E  E  U  O  R  P  H  A  L
I  M  I  S  C  O  R  V  B  U  N  V  D  V  S  B  T  I  E  R  B
C  J  N  I  E  O  I  E  A  S  A  E  A  O  L  O  R  D  R  I  R
K  T  E  D  R  D  F  N  T  E  H  S  S  C  I  T  Y  A  P  Y  V
R  E  D  B  S  E  V  I  L  O  I  Y  A  R  T  E  B  I  G  R  D
T  W  C  B  J  S  K  N  A  H  T  D  A  E  R  B  Y  U  I  L  R
U  I  N  K  W  O  U  G  T  T  A  E  S  I  I  Z  R  W  C  B  M
R  W  E  I  T  S  H  P  U  I  P  V  O  L  H  M  G  P  A  R  T
T  G  B  I  K  M  F  G  T  M  A  L  R  A  S  D  I  E  R  L  V
N  T  Q  D  N  G  I  H  P  E  S  E  S  U  J  L  B  N  D  E  H
T  U  E  C  G  L  K  A  L  S  S  W  Y  H  M  M  U  K  C  E  S
W  A  B  N  T  I  R  B  O  N  O  T  U  V  R  G  N  T  R  O  A
C  U  R  T  M  L  U  F  E  O  V  N  Y  U  O  R  I  H  J  M  C
R  A  D  B  P  Z  M  A  N  T  E  M  W  O  E  E  D  G  B  N  X
L  T  A  S  W  P  R  E  P  A  R  A  T  I  O  N  T  Y  N  B  L
```

Word Bank

FIRST	FEAST	UNLEAVENED	BLOOD (2)	DISCIPLE(S)	JESUS
PREPARATION(S)	PASSOVER	EAT	CITY	MAN	TEACHER
TIME	CELEBRATE	HOUSE	EVENING	TABLE (2)	TWELVE
TRUTH	BETRAY	SAD	NOT (2)	LORD	HYMN
TELL	COVENANT	ME (6)	THIS	CERTAIN	OLIVES
IS (2)	GAVE	DIPPED	RECLINE(ING)	HAND	BOWL
SON	WOE	BORN	CUP	RABBI	BREAD
THANKS					

Bonus: To discover something used at the supper, shade in the circled words.

SS2880

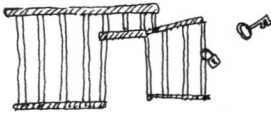

Jesus Before Pilate
Matthew 27:11-26

Read the Scripture, then circle each word from the word bank hidden in the puzzle. Words may appear forward or backwards, moving up, down, or diagonally.

```
I  W  H  I  D  E  R  E  W  S  N  A  C  C  C  Y
N  D  H  O  N  E  E  D  E  T  U  O  H  S  D  T
N  O  Y  L  P  E  R  O  Y  O  U  I  I  U  W  I
O  O  S  R  E  D  L  E  A  N  E  T  L  S  T  L
C  L  G  S  M  E  E  T  F  F  O  R  D  E  N  I
E  B  O  E  E  L  L  S  E  F  A  M  R  J  E  B
N  S  V  G  E  T  I  I  U  O  U  E  E  Y  M  I
T  D  E  D  N  A  H  N  R  C  O  S  N  G  E  S
U  E  R  U  R  B  W  G  E  A  C  S  R  N  Z  N
C  G  N  J  A  E  N  L  N  U  S  A  B  I  A  O
H  A  O  B  N  F  A  E  O  P  W  G  A  T  M  P
R  S  R  V  S  I  E  M  S  R  E  E  N  T  A  S
I  S  Y  O  R  W  M  J  I  O  J  E  S  I  U  E
S  E  S  S  A  B  B  A  R  A  B  X  X  S  K  R
T  M  X  E  T  A  L  I  P  R  M  O  T  S  U  C
```

Word Bank

MEANWHILE	HANDED	MESSAGE (2)	KING	SITTING
SUFFERED	ACCUSED	CHILDREN	AMAZEMENT	PRISONER
BARABBAS	PILATE	INNOCENT	REPLY	ANSWERED
GOVERNOR	RESPONSIBILITY	DREAM	SHOUTED	CUSTOM
ENVY	ELDERS	JESUS	UPROAR	CHIEF
JUDGE'S	CHRIST	WIFE	SINGLE	BLOOD
JEWS				

Bonus: To discover what Pilate asked the people, write the uncircled letters below. (Three X's are not used.)_____

_____

The Crucifixion

Matthew 27:32-44

Read the Scripture, then circle each word from the word bank hidden in the puzzle. Words may appear forward or backwards, moving up, down, or diagonally.

```
N C I L Y G T I N S G H A Y J E X I S
H O E W P E A N O U N C M U E T N I R
O K R M A S D S M S I T O R K S M V B
B U S F V T J U I E T A U S T U A I C
Y O C R S S T L S J S W T F J C S D T
L L A G D O G T E V A S C H I E F K E
C Y R E N E W T E A C H E R S I H I N
Y R R A C O O G R D I V I D E D E N I
N A M S S O R C P U E V E I L E B G W
B E L L Z V E G R D S S N G N P G E K
E V A M F N M O I E D T A S R M N L I
A S C L K T T L E I E O K J U O L C A
P O N I N G K G S F R L R M C H T E T
D I V D E D I O T I E U D M A G A S L
H H T L O B N T S C F P W I T R H V L
U C Y R B U T H E U F E T A I D U F I
R O O T D O B A H R O U L D C R W U E
E U N D R L A T T C S C H O Z T A N S
L R I C F I M F O R W S C T E I G N O
B S S T F F R E L O E E T B V S N J T
C T A W O I S L C B J R U R S E K O N
```

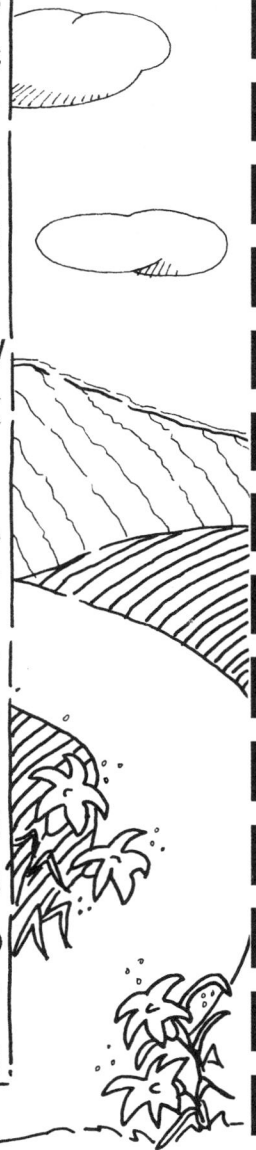

Word Bank

GO(ING)	CRUCIFIED	LEFT	HIS	UP (2)	MAN (2)	DIVIDED
INSULT(S)	CYRENE	CLOTHES	SAVE	SIMON	CASTING	CARRY
LOTS	CHIEF	CROSS	WATCH	PRIESTS	GOLGOTHA	HE (4)
TEACHERS	OFFERED	KING	BELIEVE	JESUS	JEWS	TRUST(S)
WINE	TWO	GOD	ROB(BERS)	RESCUE	GALL	

Bonus: To discover how Jesus died, shade in the circled letters.

SS2880

The Death of Jesus
Matthew 27:45-56

Read the Scripture, then circle each word from the word bank hidden in the puzzle. Words may appear forward or backwards, moving up, down, or diagonally.

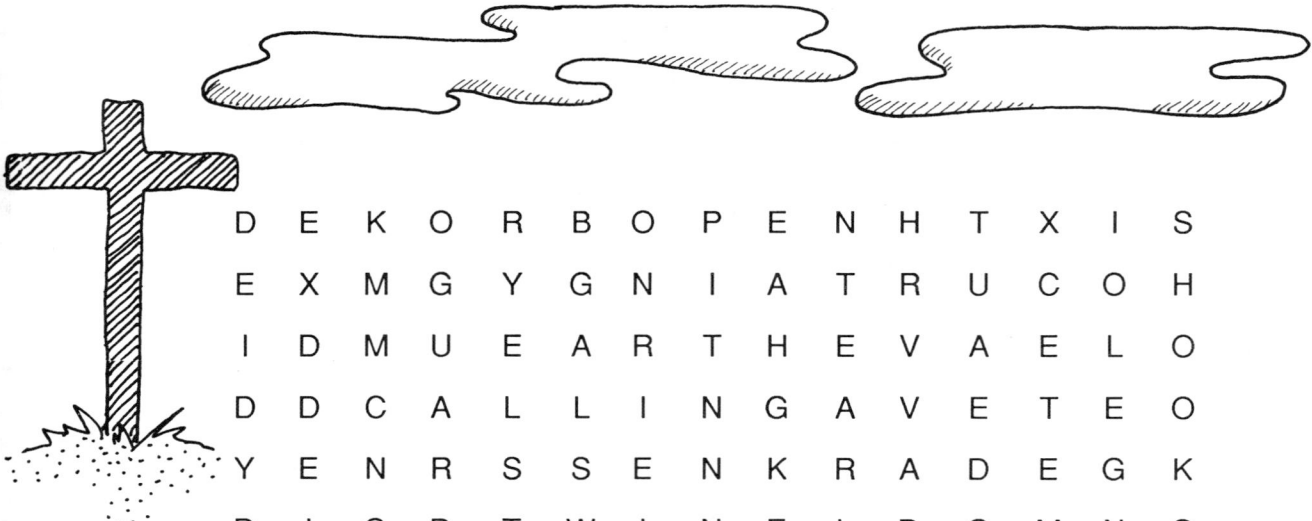

```
D E K O R B O P E N H T X I S
E X M G Y G N I A T R U C O H
I D M U E A R T H E V A E L O
D D C A L L I N G A V E T E O
Y E N R S S E N K R A D E G K
D I O D T W I N E L D G M N O
E R S I D W I H O R E Y P O G
R C C N M R H U A A I J L P N
E K A G D M D G V I F E E S I
F E S A V E E Y V S I S S A D
F L K P O N Y D O E R U E L N
O A C T I L P S I D R S I O A
U N O V O R F O C A E R D N T
S D R H A M I K E L T O O E S
H T N I N E B T N L G E B M E
```

Word Bank

SIXTH	DRINK	STICK	LEAVE	NINTH	SPIRIT
OFFERED	ALONE	CURTAIN	SON	SAVE	DARKNESS
TEMPLE	DIED	LAND	CRIED	EARTH	RAISED
JESUS	SHOOK	GUARDING	LOUD	ROCKS	TERRIFIED
VOICE	SPLIT	STANDING	TOMB(S)	GOD	BROKE
HOLY	IMMEDIATE(LY)	SPONGE	OPEN	VINEGAR	WINE
BODIES	GAVE	ALL	CALLING		

Bonus: To discover a question Jesus asked, write the uncircled letters on the lines below. (One *X* is not used.) _____

_____

The Burial of Jesus
Matthew 27:57-61

Read the Scripture, then circle each word from the word bank hidden in the puzzle. Words may appear forward or backwards, moving up, down, or diagonally.

```
D E C A L P G O H I N K G T R
O N P D I I L A T C E C T U O
N E W I H L I N E N I O A E L
A V A S S A K E D B F R P O L
M I R C J T H E R E I E P S B
E G N I N E V E U M S G R M S
D B O P D M Y N A W A Y O A U
N O C L E A N T D P B T A I S
L R L E A C H R T E E O C R E
T D O D E E M A R E C G H D J
N E T T A N A N H J O S E P H
O R H S S O R C A I M A D T I
R E T I B T Y E N E E G I V E
F D N T T S O G H I M S E L F
H B O D Y I D E P P A R W M X
```

Word Bank (words in bold)

"As **evening approached**, there **came** a **rich** man from **Arimathea**, **named Joseph**, who had **himself become** a **disciple** of **Jesus**. **Going** to **Pilate**, he asked for Jesus' **body**, and Pilate **ordered** that it be **given** to him. Joseph took the body, **wrapped** it in a **clean linen cloth**, and **placed** it in his own **new tomb** that he had cut **out** of the **rock**. He **roll**ed a **big stone** in **front** of the **entrance** to the tomb and went **away**. **Mary** Magdalene and the other Mary were **sit**ting **there across** from the tomb."   Matthew 27:57-61

Bonus: To discover what Joseph did, write the uncircled letters on the lines below. (One *X* is not used.)

_____

_____

The Resurrection
Matthew 28:1-10

Read the Scripture, then circle each word from the word bank hidden in the puzzle. Words may appear forward or backwards, moving up, down, or diagonally.

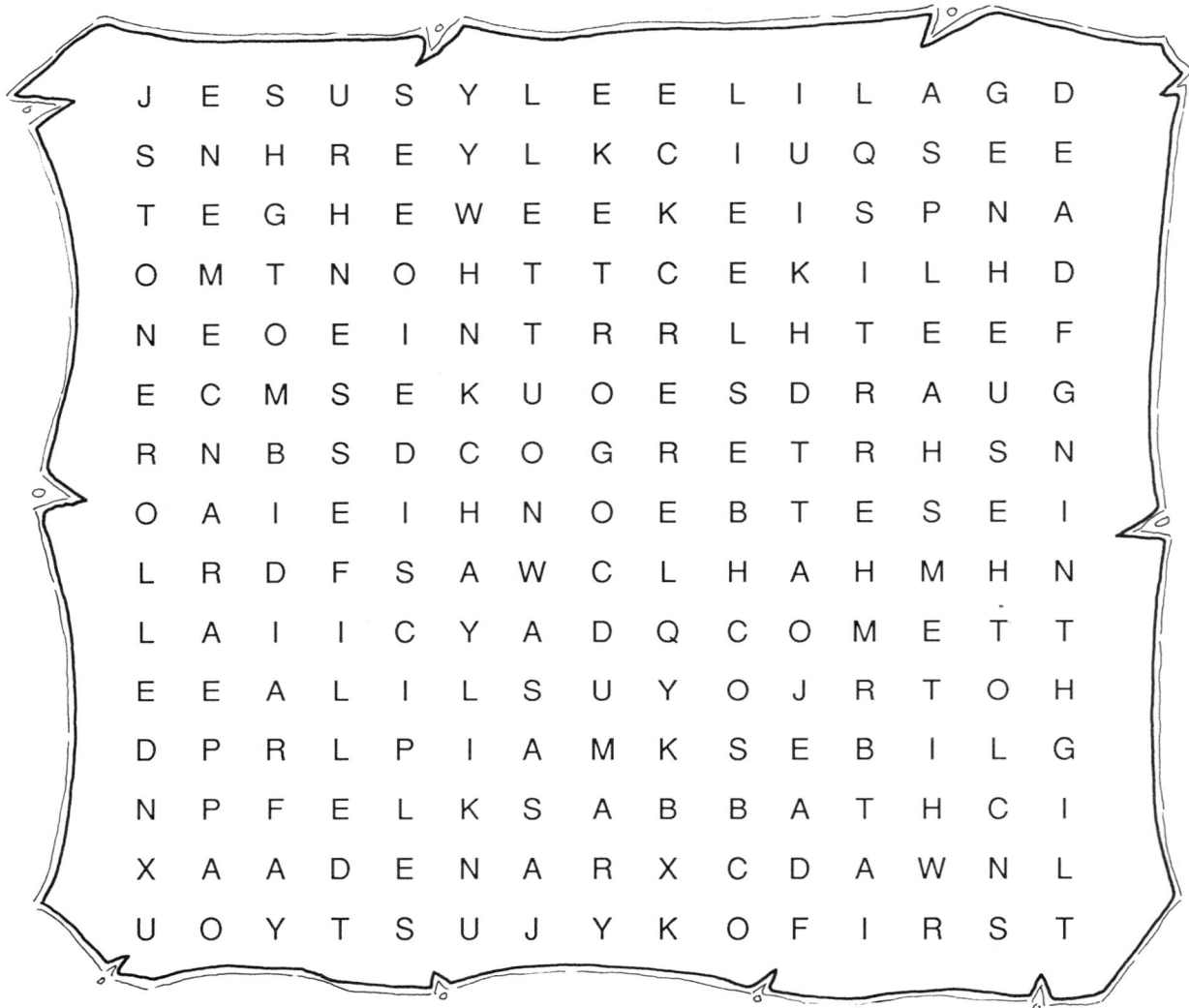

```
J  E  S  U  S  Y  L  E  E  L  I  L  A  G  D
S  N  H  R  E  Y  L  K  C  I  U  Q  S  E  E
T  E  G  H  E  W  E  E  K  E  I  S  P  N  A
O  M  T  N  O  H  T  T  C  E  K  I  L  H  D
N  E  O  E  I  N  T  R  R  L  H  T  E  E  F
E  C  M  S  E  K  U  O  E  S  D  R  A  U  G
R  N  B  S  D  C  O  G  R  E  T  R  H  S  N
O  A  I  E  I  H  N  O  E  B  T  E  S  E  I
L  R  D  F  S  A  W  C  L  H  A  H  M  H  N
L  A  I  I  C  Y  A  D  Q  C  O  M  E  T  T
E  E  A  L  I  L  S  U  Y  O  J  R  T  O  H
D  P  R  L  P  I  A  M  K  S  E  B  I  L  G
N  P  F  E  L  K  S  A  B  B  A  T  H  C  I
X  A  A  D  E  N  A  R  X  C  D  A  W  N  L
U  O  Y  T  S  U  J  Y  K  O  F  I  R  S  T
```

Word Bank

SABBATH	LIGHTNING	QUICKLY	DAWN	FIRST
WHITE	CLOTHES	DISCIPLES	RISEN	DAY
GUARDS	DEAD	WEEK	AFRAID	FEET
MARY	SHOOK	FILLED	TOMB	LOOKING
JOY	EARTHQUAKE	JESUS	WORSHIPED	GALILEE
CRUCIFIED	ROLLED	BROTHERS	STONE	MEN (2)
COME	SEE (2)	APPEARANCE	PLACE	MET
TELL	LIKE	YOU	BACK	RAN
ANGEL	THEY	JUST	HIS	DO

Bonus: To discover the angel's message, write the uncircled letters on the lines below. (Two *X*'s are not used.) _____

_____

The Great Commission
Matthew 28:16-20

Read the Scripture, then circle each word from the word bank hidden in the puzzle. Words may appear forward or backwards, moving up, down, or diagonally.

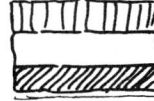

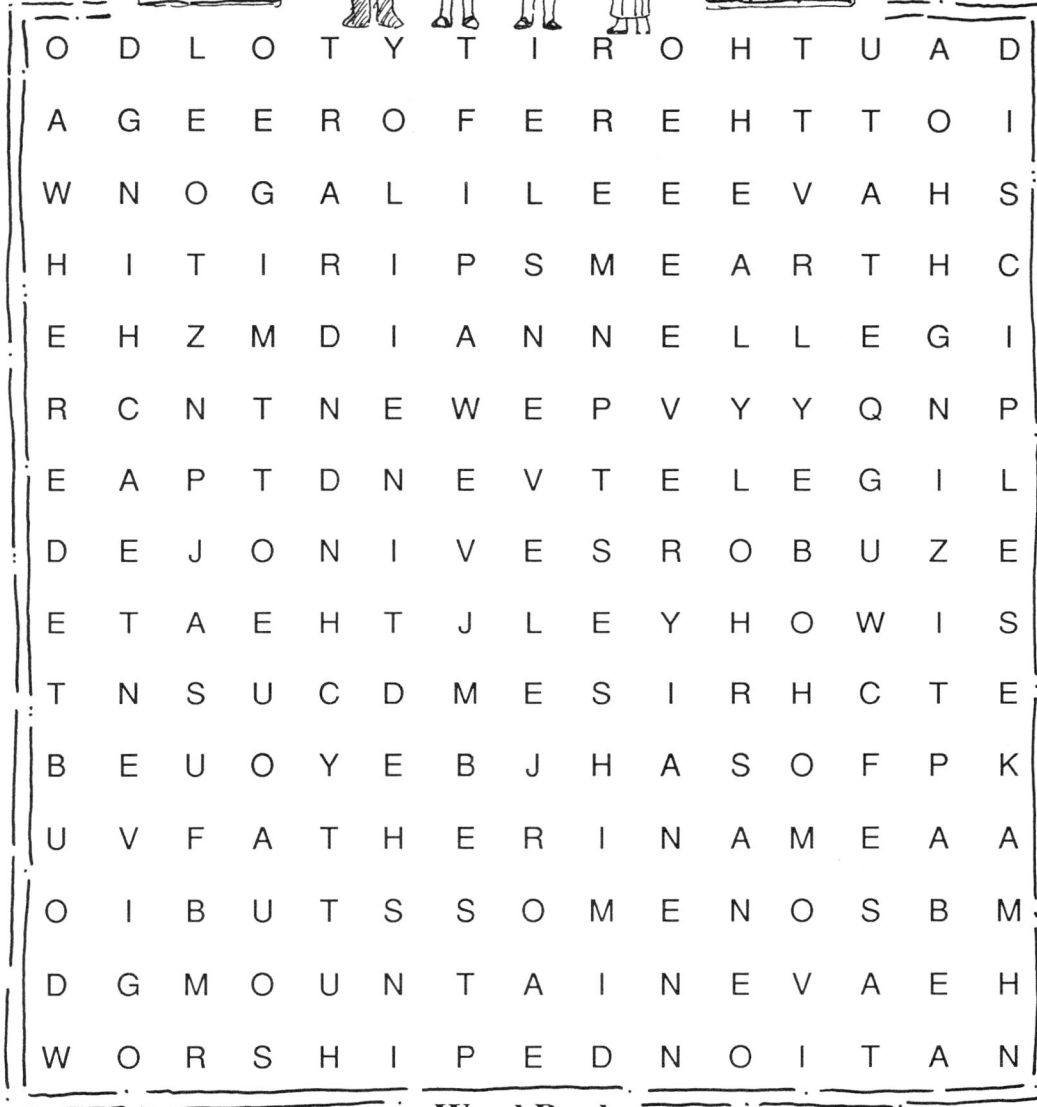

```
O D L O T Y T I R O H T U A D
A G E E R O F E R E H T T O I
W N O G A L I L E E E V A H S
H I T I R I P S M E A R T H C
E H Z M D I A N N E L L E G I
R C N T N E W E P V Y Y Q N P
E A P T D N E V T E L E G I L
D E J O N I V E S R O B U Z E
E T A E H T J L E Y H O W I S
T N S U C D M E S I R H C T E
B E U O Y E B J H A S O F P K
U V F A T H E R I N A M E A A
O I B U T S S O M E N O S B M
D G M O U N T A I N E V A E H
W O R S H I P E D N O I T A N
```

Word Bank

THE	WHERE	HEAVEN	VERY	ELEVEN	EARTH
END	DISCIPLES	THEREFORE	TO (8)	GALILEE	NATION(S)
AGE	MOUNTAIN	BAPTIZING	GO (5)	OF (2)	YOU
JESUS	BE (6)	MAKE	HIM	TOLD	FATHER
HAS	BUT	THEM	SON	HOLY	WORSHIPED
SPIRIT	SOME	TEACHING	DOUBTED	AUTHORITY	OBEY
NAME	GIVEN	WENT	HAVE		

Bonus: To discover the main message of the Great Commission, shade in the uncircled letters.

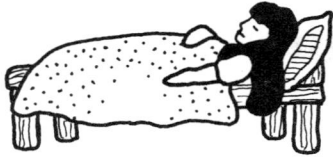

Jairus' Daughter
Mark 5:21-24, 35-43

Read the Scripture, then circle each word from the word bank hidden in the puzzle. Words may appear forward or backwards, moving up, down, or diagonally.

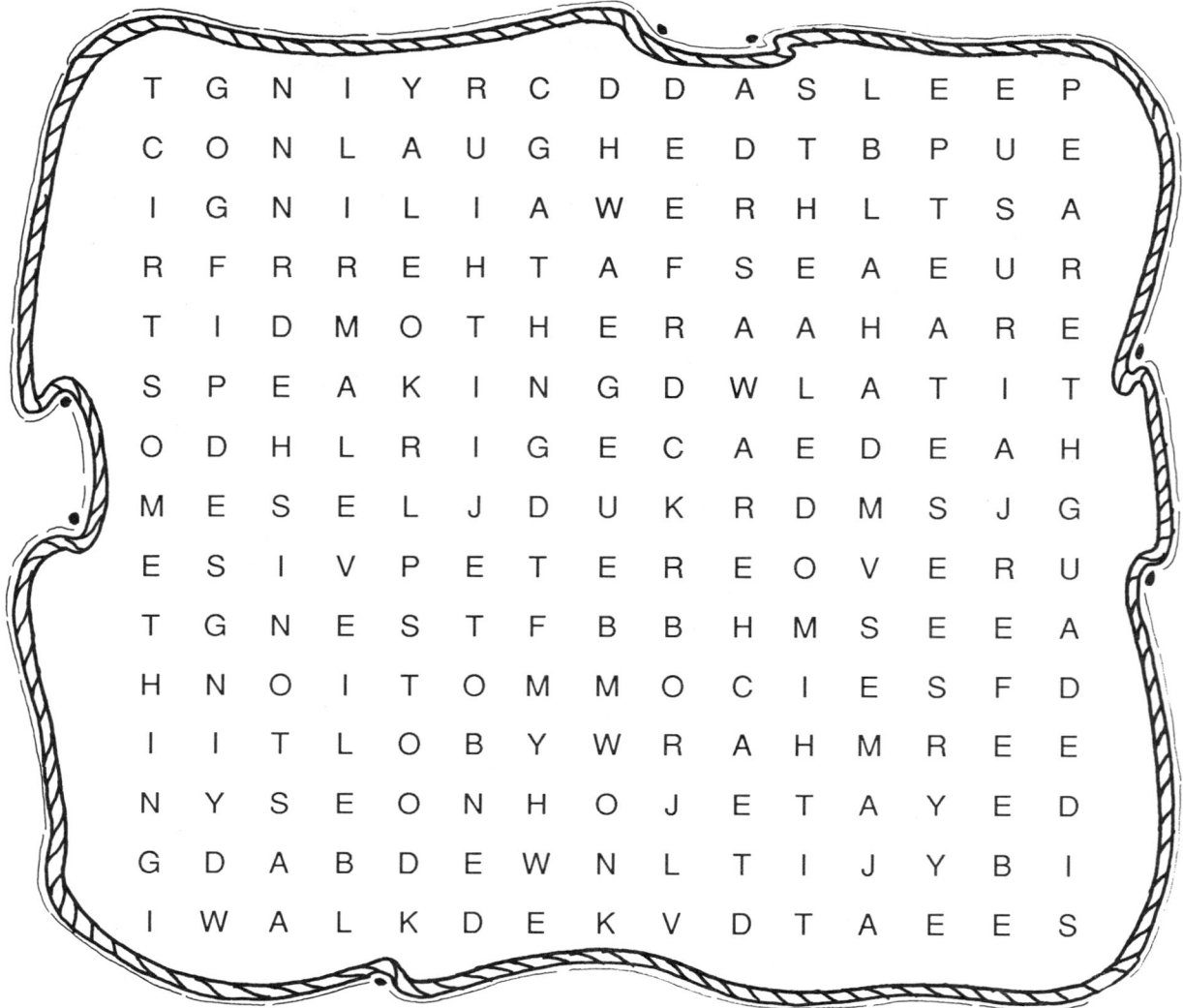

```
T G N I Y R C D D A S L E E P
C O N L A U G H E D T B P U E
I G N I L I A W E R H L T S A
R F R R E H T A F S E A E U R
T I D M O T H E R A A H A R E
S P E A K I N G D W L A T I T
O D H L R I G E C A E D E A H
M E S E L J D U K R D M S J G
E S I V P E T E R E O V E R U
T G N E S T F B B H M S E E A
H N O I T O M M O C I E S F D
I I T L O B Y W R A H M R E E
N Y S E O N H O J E T A Y E D
G D A B D E W N L T I J Y B I
I W A L K D E K V D T A E E S
```

Word Bank

OVER	SPEAKING	ASLEEP	CROSSED	TEACHER
LAUGHED	BOAT	SIDE	AFRAID	MOTHER
LAKE	BELIEVE	FATHER	CROWD	PETER
STOOD	GATHERED	JAMES	WALK(ED)	JAIRUS
JOHN	ASTONISHED	FELL	HOME	STRICT
PLEADED	COMMOTION	DAUGHTER	CRYING	KNOW
DYING	WAILING	SOMETHING	HEALED	EAT (2)
PUT	OF	SEE(ING) (3)	GIRL	HAD
HIM (2)	WAS	WHY	BY (3)	HE (6)

Bonus: To discover what Jesus said, write the uncircled letters on the lines below. _____

_____

_____

Shining Star Publications. Copyright © 1993

SS2880

Jesus and the Children
Mark 10:13-16

Read the Scripture, then circle each word from the word bank hidden in the puzzle. Words may appear forward or backwards, moving up, down, or diagonally.

```
A  P  N  D  A  H  E  B  B  T  T  R  U  T  H
O  E  O  K  R  T  L  H  E  E  C  H  R  H  A
I  O  L  D  M  E  R  E  N  I  L  N  E  H  N
I  P  D  I  S  C  I  P  L  E  S  O  T  M  D
S  L  A  S  R  E  M  O  C  M  E  S  N  P  S
U  E  E  T  L  H  T  O  O  K  V  H  E  G  I
S  D  G  N  I  G  N  I  R  B  I  T  T  H  S
C  A  N  D  T  H  E  M  E  S  E  O  N  U  S
H  C  U  O  T  O  R  R  B  U  C  N  A  A  P
I  N  N  E  L  R  D  E  U  C  E  T  N  H  E
L  M  L  T  E  H  L  D  K  H  R  Y  G  A  N
D  L  H  V  T  I  I  N  E  D  O  W  I  X  L
B  I  E  H  K  S  H  I  D  N  L  H  D  E  E
S  N  E  E  S  S  C  H  E  E  D  O  N  T  T
S  U  S  E  J  H  E  M  O  D  G  N  I  K  M
```

Word Bank (words in bold)

"**People** were **bringing little children** to **Jesus** to have him **touch them**, but **the disciples rebuked** them. When Jesus saw **this**, he was **indignant**. He said to them, '**Let the** little children **come** to **me,** and do **not hinder** them, for the **kingdom** of **God belongs** to **such** as these. I **tell** you the **truth, anyone who** will **not receive** the kingdom of God **like** a little **child** will **never enter** it.' And he **took** the children in **his arms**, **put his hands** on them and **blessed them.**" Mark 10:13-16

Bonus: To discover what Jesus did to the children, write the uncircled letters on the lines below. (One X is not used.) _____

_____

SS2880

Blind Bartimaeus
Mark 10:46-52

Read the Scripture, then circle each word from the word bank hidden in the puzzle. Words may appear forward or backwards, moving up, down, or diagonally.

```
F  S  G  D  S  E  O  E  D  I  S  D  A  O  R
E  Y  O  G  I  E  T  M  O  R  E  O  S  U  R
E  Y  E  N  G  S  C  H  E  E  R  C  I  T  Y
T  L  G  I  H  F  C  Y  R  O  A  D  D  R  A
K  E  R  G  T  I  E  I  I  O  T  E  E  E  H
A  T  A  G  R  H  H  T  P  H  W  V  W  H  G
O  A  L  E  T  G  T  H  Y  L  A  I  A  T  N
L  I  J  B  D  N  E  E  C  C  E  E  N  E  I
C  D  S  H  E  I  R  N  R  A  N  C  T  G  T
E  E  A  J  P  V  A  D  E  L  A  E  H  O  T
I  M  D  E  M  A  Z  L  M  L  M  R  F  T  I
B  M  N  S  U  E  A  M  I  T  R  A  B  O  S
B  I  I  U  J  L  N  D  A  V  I  D  E  U  R
A  D  L  S  H  O  U  T  Y  T  E  I  U  Q  T
R  E  B  U  K  E  D  O  H  U  D  W  O  R  C
```

Word Bank

JERICHO	BARTIMAEUS	CALL	THEN	SITTING	CHEER
THEY	ROADSIDE	FEET	JESUS	BEGGING	THROWING
DISCIPLE(S)	NAZARETH	CLOAK	TOGETHER	SHOUT	ASIDE
LARGE	DAVID	JUMPED	CROWD	MERCY	RABBI
LEAVING	REBUKED	WANT	CITY	QUIET	FAITH
BLIND	MORE	HEALED	MAN	SON	RECEIVED
SIGHT	IMMEDIATELY	ROAD	SEE	BUT	FOR

Bonus: To discover what Jesus told Bartimaeus, write the uncircled letters on the lines below.

_____

_____

SS2880

The Triumphal Entry
Mark 11:1-11

Read the Scripture, then circle each word from the word bank hidden in the puzzle. Words may appear forward or backwards, moving up, down or diagonally.

```
B  E  T  H  A  N  Y  T  T  C  E  A  H  E  A  D  O  W  T
E  J  M  R  K  L  J  I  N  O  L  I  V  E  S  L  O  R  D
T  M  C  A  R  P  Q  E  E  L  P  C  E  M  K  I  M  E  N
H  B  N  T  W  U  L  B  S  T  I  D  B  O  C  N  E  T  E
P  A  C  M  K  Y  T  J  R  U  C  B  V  N  R  U  A  N  D
H  R  B  S  R  T  L  L  P  I  S  V  Y  E  I  Z  M  E  D
A  W  S  M  V  R  M  J  R  Z  I  K  I  N  L  O  H  W  I
G  O  B  T  H  S  M  F  G  H  D  M  O  S  E  Z  C  D  R
E  H  T  Z  R  I  S  D  C  N  B  A  C  K  T  N  U  O  M
C  O  M  E  C  O  R  T  R  G  E  L  P  O  E  P  Y  O  D
K  D  T  I  H  U  J  E  D  X  C  L  O  A  K  S  E  R  E
I  I  U  T  G  L  A  T  E  Y  U  M  B  P  L  Y  H  W  E
N  V  B  R  I  N  G  M  G  P  O  M  S  C  R  S  T  A  N
G  A  B  W  H  U  O  L  A  E  N  H  U  K  M  J  R  Y  A
D  D  L  U  S  N  F  M  L  V  A  R  T  S  U  B  U  J  N
O  U  T  W  R  Q  Z  V  L  T  X  B  E  W  R  S  J  C  N
M  R  M  E  T  C  U  M  I  O  E  S  P  L  E  M  T  D  A
K  O  O  L  G  E  R  S  V  A  R  E  B  W  P  F  D  E  S
S  A  R  S  T  T  N  N  D  N  I  F  R  Z  M  R  E  S  O
A  D  S  E  H  C  N  A  R  B  J  U  S  T  D  B  M  O  H
A  P  P  R  O  A  C  H  E  D  M  E  L  A  S  U  R  E  J
```

Word Bank

JERUSALEM	BETHPHAGE	BETHANY	MOUNT	OLIVES	JESUS
SENT	TWO	DISCIPLE	VILLAGE	AHEAD	ENTER
FIND	ARE	TO (6)	COLT	TIE(D) (2)	RIDDEN
LORD	NEED(S)	BRING	BACK	STREET	DOORWAY
PEOPLE	CLOAKS	ROAD	BUT	OUT	BRANCHES
HOSANNA	GO (2)	THE	ASK(S) (2)	HE (4)	AND
WHY	KINGDOM	JUST	DAVID	IT (6)	HIGH(EST)
LATE	OF	COME(S)	AS (3)	WHO	LOOK(ED)
APPROACHED	THEY				

Bonus: Shade in the uncircled letters to find the shape of something the people threw down.

Shining Star Publications, Copyright © 1993

SS2880

The Greatest Commandment
Mark 12:28-34

Read the Scripture, then circle each word from the word bank hidden in the puzzle. Words may appear forward or backwards, moving up, down, or diagonally.

```
T  R  A  E  H  R  E  P  L  I  E  D  D  E  R
N  E  I  G  H  B  O  R  E  S  I  W  O  A  D
S  G  O  D  F  L  E  S  R  U  O  Y  C  S  R
R  T  E  A  C  H  E  R  D  N  A  H  T  U  O
E  I  N  G  N  I  T  A  B  E  D  T  S  X  L
W  T  H  E  M  O  D  L  U  R  N  G  E  R  M
S  N  O  N  M  T  I  L  R  A  W  N  Q  N  O
N  A  S  K  E  D  X  U  N  M  L  E  U  E  G
A  T  C  M  R  E  N  P  T  E  O  R  E  V  N
E  R  L  O  W  K  Y  A  F  I  V  T  S  I  I
R  O  V  N  A  I  O  M  M  S  E  S  T  G  C
C  P  Q  E  L  M  U  O  L  M  D  N  I  M  I
R  M  O  P  A  L  R  R  U  O  O  F  O  X  T
U  I  S  R  A  E  L  E  O  S  O  C  N  H  O
R  M  P  D  N  O  C  E  S  T  H  E  S  E  N
```

Word Bank

ONE (2)	ISRAEL	BURNT	TEACHER	LORD
TO (7)	LAW	GOD	MORE (2)	IN (2)
LOVE	WISE(LY)	AND	DEBATING	HEART
YOUR	SOUL	IS (4)	GIVEN	MIND
STRENGTH	HE(3)	QUESTIONS	ANSWER	SECOND
ASKED	OF (3)	NO (6)	COMMANDMENTS	NEIGHBOR
THESE	THEM	MOST	YOURSELF	NOTICING
IMPORTANT	ALL	ARE	REPLIED	AS (2)

Bonus: To discover how we should treat others, shade in the uncircled letters. (Three *X*'s are not used.)

SS2880

Jesus Predicts Peter's Denial
Mark 14:27-31

Read the Scripture, then circle each word from the word bank hidden in the puzzle. Words may appear forward or backwards, moving up, down, or diagonally.

```
B  H  E  I  D  E  S  H  E  P  H  E  R  D  F
O  R  T  A  H  E  A  D  R  N  E  V  E  E  E
N  Y  P  U  T  D  J  E  O  H  L  E  X  C  S
W  O  E  R  R  E  O  R  F  L  A  E  O  L  W
O  U  E  S  S  T  T  E  E  E  M  F  R  A  O
S  R  H  U  Y  S  C  T  B  P  R  O  T  R  R
I  S  S  W  A  I  S  T  H  W  T  O  O  E  C
D  E  R  E  W  S  N  A  W  R  N  O  L  D  R
S  L  E  I  A  N  T  C  C  I  S  E  L  E  Y
R  F  E  O  U  I  O  S  G  T  Y  M  I  I  E
E  A  L  R  C  W  N  H  E  T  I  A  W  N  C
H  L  I  A  E  L  T  R  H  E  I  S  D  T  I
T  L  L  D  L  T  D  R  I  N  S  M  I  O  W
O  L  A  R  I  S  E  N  O  R  E  V  E  N  T
Y  W  G  N  M  E  E  P  E  K  I  R  T  S  X
```

Word Bank

FALL	PETER	ROOSTER	AWAY	DECLARED
CROWS	JESUS	EVEN	TWICE	WRITTEN
EMPHATICALLY	WILL	YOURSELF	STRIKE	NOT (2)
DISOWN	SHEPHERD	TELL	THREE	SHEEP
TRUTH	TIMES	SCATTERED	ANSWERED	INSISTED
AFTER	TODAY	RISEN	TONIGHT	DIE (3)
NEVER	AHEAD	INTO	OTHERS	GALILEE
BEFORE	SAME			

Bonus: To discover what Peter was going to do, write the uncircled letters on the lines below. (Two X's are not used.) _____

_____

Gethsemane
Mark 14:32-42

Read the Scripture, then circle each word from the word bank hidden in the puzzle. Words may appear forward or backwards, moving up, down, or diagonally.

```
P O S S I B L E K A E W O H S
B E V I D N U O F T B H G T W
E V E E P S I M O N E E R A I
G E E E R W H G J G T R P E L
A R C K A W G O I H R E U D L
N Y G A Y X H L S W A T C H I
O T R T L N H E A V Y E D G N
I H O Y E P M S L E E P I N G
T I U L I A S P Y M D R S I C
A N N P N U A D A S E P C N A
T G D E S S E R T S I D I R L
P H Y E Y E S I S R X N P U L
M O J D D N A H I F A L L T E
E U L U O S I T X Y L P E E D
T R O U B L E D J A M E S R X
```

Word Bank

PLACE	TROUBLED	SIMON	DISTRESSED	CALLED	SOUL
FALL	BETRAYED	GETHSEMANE	OVERWHELMED	TEMPTATION	HAND(S)
JESUS	DEATH	SPIRIT	SIN(NERS)	DISCIPLES	STAY
WILLING	SIT	WATCH	BODY	GO (5)	PRAY
GROUND	WEAK	PETER	HOUR	EYES	JAMES
EVERYTHING	HEAVY	JOHN	POSSIBLE	RETURNING	BEGAN
TAKE	THIRD	DEEPLY (2)	CUP	SLEEPING	FOUND

Bonus: To discover what Jesus told His disciples, write the uncircled letters on the lines below. (Four X's are not used.) _____

_____

The Birth of John the Baptist
Luke 1:57-66

Read the Scripture, then circle each word from the word bank hidden in the puzzle. Words may appear forward or backwards, moving up, down, or diagonally.

```
Y  O  J  S  I  G  N  S  A  I  D  F  I  N  D  T
N  A  M  E  N  N  E  O  Z  T  H  A  T  S  O  N
G  R  E  A  T  H  K  E  E  I  H  T  H  G  I  E
M  O  M  D  D  L  I  H  C  S  T  H  A  N  D  M
O  E  I  B  U  L  L  I  H  E  C  E  H  T  Y  H
A  M  R  N  L  J  L  Y  A  D  O  R  T  E  L  S
D  I  T  C  G  J  H  D  R  E  H  T  O  M  E  I
N  T  E  E  Y  H  T  R  I  B  W  O  N  E  T  N
E  O  H  W  L  H  E  A  A  G  O  D  G  G  A  O
I  V  S  R  A  B  B  E  H  G  E  N  U  N  I  T
G  O  I  I  E  A  A  H  L  S  N  J  E  I  D  S
H  P  H  T  R  B  Z  T  O  R  R  O  N  S  E  A
B  E  T  I  A  Y  I  O  R  O  E  H  M  I  M  L
O  N  U  N  H  L  L  X  D  F  H  N  X  A  M  L
R  E  O  G  S  P  E  S  I  C  M  U  C  R  I  C
S  D  M  A  D  E  U  R  X  E  V  A  G  P  P  U
```

Word Bank

ELIZABETH	CIRCUMCISE	MOUTH	BABY	CHILD	TONGUE
BIRTH	FATHER	LOOSED	SON	ZECHARIAH	PRAISING
MOTHER	GOD	NEIGHBORS	RELATIVE(S)	JOHN	AWE
LORD	AMONG	HILL	GREAT	HER	JUDEA
MERCY	SIGNS	HAND	JOY	DAY	WRITING
EIGHTH	TABLET	TIME	THE	UP (2)	SHE
ASTONISHMENT	SAID	FOR	THAT	MADE	GAVE
IMMEDIATELY	LIKE	OPENED	WHO	HEARD	NAME (2)
SHARE(D)	FIND	ALL	ONE (2)	GOING	

Bonus: To discover what Zechariah said, write the uncircled letters on the lines below. (Three *X*'s are not used.) _____

_____

  SS2880

The Boy Jesus at the Temple

Luke 2:41-52

Read the Scripture, then circle each word from the word bank hidden in the puzzle. Words may appear forward or backwards, moving up, down, or diagonally.

```
T Z A C C O R I N G B O J E R U S L M A N S E A P
U F N S G N D E B Y G M E N T R E S U T D T S N A
N T A P M A Y C U S T H R E E P A S I T L L R U S
M A Z D T R S I L J E S U S O N A D Z A M A O F E
I N A D U H R E Y E A R S C O U R T F O U N M O S
P B R V A M I H R E H T A F B R O V A F R K O N N
J S E K O O L T R A V E L R E H T O M T U P P E Y
H T S H E T S A E F R I E N D S B O Y O N L B E A
Y E T E R G D Q V E H O M E I O S M U H D I E L E
R A N A U W O S E Z T V X V E V L Y N E E S H I N
D C E R T A D U R C E E C E N U A L D R R T I H R
I H R D A R E S O C R R O R T T R A S T S E N W A
N E A S T N L F N D A E M Y D A C T T S T N D O S
A R P E S G E O F I Z W P N N T H A D R A I N N P
C S A V N S A N A N A S A S U S I V G H N N I K V
N M S I O O W R Y R N N N E O O W N S M D G F T T
P O S T I E D U M B D A Y A F S Z D N D I N E R N
Q T O A T R W V S T E H E R M R M B A F N O L E F
W S V L S H E E L D V O R C E H O H N N G M P A D
F U E E E T V L A I L U A H W C S S W U Y A M S Z
L C R R U A L T S E E S W I E A U N E O A T E U N
O D O G Q F E R U N W E A N R E W T R C S O T R V
K A M A Z E D S I T T I N G G N I D R O C C A E E
Y E N O Y R E V E D L O U Y A S T O N I S H E D T
M O D S I W N E M K C A B F I N D O B E D I E N T
T R E A T E D Y L S U O I X N A G N I N R U T E R
```

Word Bank

EVERYONE	TREASURED	SAY(ING) (2)	KNOW	OVER	PARENTS
TRAVEL(ED)	SON	JERUSALEM	DAY	TO (15)	HOUSE
FATHER	FEAST	TREATED	MOTHER	PASSOVER	ME (5)
FRIENDS	NAZARETH	TWELVE	LOOK	OBEDIENT (2)	FOUND
YEARS	THREE	HEART	OLD	TEMPLE	ACCORDING
WISDOM	CUSTOM	COURT	STATURE	HOME	BEHIND
TEACHERS	FAVOR	BOY	QUESTIONS	GOD	UP
JESUS	HEARD	MEN (2)	COMPANY	AMAZED	FIND (2)
LISTENING	ANSWER(S)	SITTING	EVERY	SEARCHING	UNAWARE
AMONG	UNDERSTANDING	ASTONISHED	BACK	AND (3)	WHILE
GREW	HIM	RETURNING	ANXIOUSLY	RELATIVES	

Bonus: To see where Jesus went, shade in the uncircled letters. (One *X* is not used.)

The Temptation of Jesus
Luke 4:1-13

Read the Scripture, then circle each word from the word bank hidden in the puzzle. Words may appear forward or backwards, moving up, down, or diagonally.

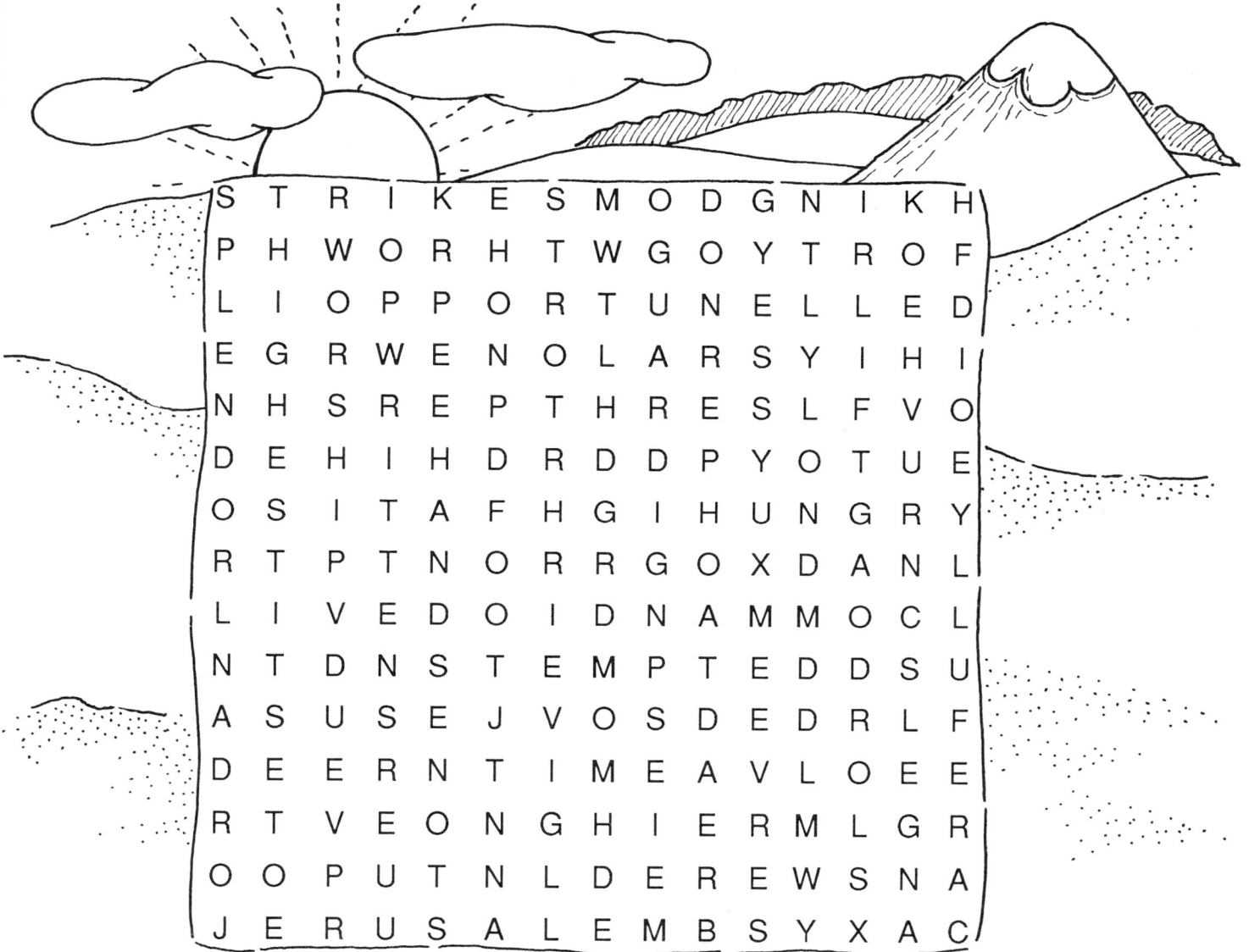

```
S T R I K E S M O D G N I K H
P H W O R H T W G O Y T R O F
L I O P P O R T U N E L L E D
E G R W E N O L A R S Y I H I
N H S R E P T H R E S L F V O
D E H I H D R D D P Y O T U E
O S I T A F H G I H U N G R Y
R T P T N O R R G O X D A N L
L I V E D O I D N A M M O C L
N T D N S T E M P T E D D S U
A S U S E J V O S D E D R L F
D E E R N T I M E A V L O E E
R T V E O N G H I E R M L G R
O O P U T N L D E R E W S N A
J E R U S A L E M B S Y X A C
```

Word Bank

JESUS	BREAD	WORSHIP	GUARD	HOLY SPIRIT	ANSWERED	LORD
CAREFULLY	WRITTEN	GOD	LIFT	JORDAN	LED	SERVE
PUT	ALONE	JERUSALEM	HANDS	FORTY	HIGH	HIGHEST
STRIKE	POINT	FOOT	TEMPTED	LIVE	SHOWED	TEST
OPPORTUNE	TIME	THROW	COMMAND	ANGELS	HUNGRY	STONE
TELL	KINGDOMS	GIVE	SPLENDOR	LIVED		

Bonus: To discover what Jesus said to Satan, write the uncircled letters on the lines below. (Two *X* 's are not used.) _____

_____

Jesus Calms the Storms
Luke 8:22-25

Read the Scripture, then circle each word from the word bank hidden in the puzzle. Words may appear forward or backwards, moving up, down, or diagonally.

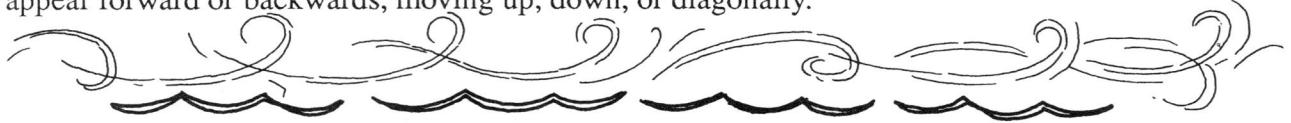

```
D  W  B  H  R  E  H  T  O  N  A  K  S  A
I  R  E  B  U  K  E  D  M  E  O  U  T  R
A  E  I  T  E  S  D  E  D  I  S  B  U  S
S  G  N  E  V  E  H  I  M  E  H  T  Q  H
S  N  G  M  L  A  C  E  J  I  N  U  I  I
T  A  T  O  G  D  W  O  K  E  A  R  G  S
O  D  N  I  W  E  R  E  M  L  L  A  O  E
R  S  W  Y  O  L  U  E  L  M  L  E  I  L
M  T  A  H  T  I  Z  H  T  I  A  F  N  P
B  R  T  E  K  A  L  F  W  A  S  N  G  I
O  N  E  K  M  S  S  A  E  I  L  I  D  C
A  F  R  A  G  I  N  G  N  Y  E  B  O  S
T  E  S  L  D  D  Y  I  T  A  E  R  G  I
A  L  D  E  P  M  A  W  S  I  P  A  N  D
T  L  N  W  O  R  D  H  M  A  S  T  E  R
```

Word Bank (in bold letters)

"**One day Jesus said** to his **disciples**, 'Let's go over to the other **side** of the **lake**.' So they **got** into a **boat** and **set** (2) **out**. As they **sailed**, he **fell asleep**. A **squall** came down on the **lake**, so **that** the boat was **being swamped**, and they **were** in **great danger**. The disciples **went** and **woke him**, saying, '**Master**, Master, we're **going** to **drown**!' He got up and **rebuked** the **wind and** the **raging waters**; the **storm subsided**, and **all** (3) **was calm**. 'Where is your **faith**?' he **asked his** disciples. **In** (7) **fear** and **amazement** they asked one **another**, 'Who is this? He **commands even** the winds **and** the water, and they **obey him**.'"

Luke 8:22-25

Bonus: To discover what Jesus asked His disciples, write the uncircled letters on the line below.

_____

Shining Star Publications. Copyright © 1993

SS2880

Mary and Martha
Luke 10:38-42

Read the Scripture, then circle each word from the word bank hidden in the puzzle. Words may appear forward or backwards, moving up, down, or diagonally.

```
Y  P  L  E  H  M  Y  S  E  L  F  M  B  A  F
A  R  I  Y  A  D  I  S  C  I  P  L  E  S  E
W  H  S  R  A  S  C  N  H  O  S  E  T  E  E
N  W  T  H  N  E  S  O  H  C  A  D  T  T  T
I  H  E  M  O  H  S  I  B  E  I  A  E  T  T
A  E  N  N  E  K  A  T  R  S  A  M  R  N  D
I  T  I  H  L  W  W  A  T  H  I  N  G  S  I
Y  T  N  E  O  L  L  R  N  E  E  D  E  D  O
R  E  G  R  R  N  A  A  L  L  E  T  O  T  P
A  S  K  E  D  C  B  P  V  I  L  L  A  G  E
M  P  E  T  T  A  D  E  R  E  W  S  N  A  N
S  U  S  E  J  K  S  R  E  N  O  H  A  W  E
A  Y  D  R  F  H  O  P  C  A  M  E  I  R  D
Y  A  W  A  E  W  A  Y  O  M  A  H  E  M  R
E  M  A  C  S  I  S  T  E  R  N  T  F  E  L
```

Word Bank (in bold letters)

"As **Jesus** and his **disciples** were on their **way** (2), he **came** to a **village** where a **woman** named **Martha opened** her **home** to **him**. **She** (3) had a **sister** called **Mary**, who sat at the **Lord**'s **feet listening** to what he said. But Martha was **distracted** by all the **preparations** that had to be **made**. She **came** to him and **asked**, 'Lord, don't you **care** that my sister has **left** me to do the **work** by **myself**? **Tell her** to **help** me!' 'Martha, Martha,' the Lord **answered**, 'you are **worried** and **upset** about many **things**, but only one thing is **needed**. Mary has **chosen** what is **better**, and it will not be **taken away** from her.'"   Luke 10:38-42

Bonus: To discover what Jesus said about Mary, write the uncircled letters on the lines below.

_____

_____

Zacchaeus
Luke 19:1-10

Read the Scripture, then circle each word from the word bank hidden in the puzzle. Words may appear forward or backwards, moving up, down, or diagonally.

```
C  E  B  N  O  I  S  E  S  S  O  P  E  M  S
A  C  T  R  E  E  Y  A  P  A  W  A  S  T  A
M  D  T  A  E  H  C  Y  B  L  V  R  B  C  L
E  O  Y  H  T  L  A  E  W  V  M  E  M  H  U
F  W  E  L  C  O  M  E  D  A  A  T  I  I  T
E  N  X  A  T  R  O  H  S  T  N  T  L  E  O
B  S  U  S  E  J  R  E  V  I  G  U  C  F  M
C  D  H  A  L  F  E  P  O  O  R  M  I  O  E
T  L  F  E  P  A  S  S  I  N  G  G  M  M  T
L  T  U  G  I  P  E  O  I  L  R  M  B  C  S
A  W  E  A  L  M  M  S  F  M  S  S  A  P  D
E  N  X  O  D  R  O  L  O  S  T  R  E  M  Y
S  Y  C  R  O  T  C  E  L  L  O  C  N  A  P
```

Word Bank

JESUS	PASSING	CHIEF	COLLECTOR	TAX
WEALTHY	SHORT	CLIMB (ED)	SYCAMORE	FIG
TREE	SO (7)	IF	COME	DOWN
WELCOMED	SAW	MUTTER	SIN(NER)	LORD
MAN	BY	HALF	POSSESSION(S)	POOR
CHEAT(ED)	PAY	SALVATION	SAVE	LOST
HE (7)	GIVE			

Bonus: To see what Zacchaeus climbed, shade in the circled letters.

SS2880

Judas Agrees to Betray Jesus
Luke 22:1-6

Read the Scripture, then circle each word from the word bank hidden in the puzzle. Words may appear forward or backwards, moving up, down, or diagonally.

```
            X  D  W  O  N  T  X
      S  A  W  A  U  X  B  O  H  D  X
      C  O  N  S  E  N  T  E  D  A  E  X  E
      C  X  A  E  T  R  L  E  T  A  N  L  Y  L  N
   X  R  T  F  V  E  B  E  N  R  G  D  I  A  P  F  O
J  F  O  O  R  L  A  S  A  T  A  N  R  G  W  M  M  A
O  U  W  I  A  E  C  N  V  E  Y  I  E  H  T  E  O  G
F  X  D  R  I  W  H  E  E  R  R  K  V  T  D  T  N  R
R  I  D  A  D  T  E  H  N  E  E  O  O  E  E  I  E  E
F  F  O  C  S  O  R  W  E  D  V  O  S  D  H  X  Y  E
D  E  S  S  U  C  S  I  D  X  O  L  S  C  C  A  N  D
X  A  I  I  X  P  E  O  P  L  E  F  A  O  T  N  E  W
X  S  E  H  S  R  E  C  I  F  F  O  P  H  A  N  D  X
   T  N  O  C  A  L  L  E  D  R  A  U  G  W  A  L
      H  S  T  S  E  I  R  P  X  T  H  G  I  M
         E  O  R  O  F  P  R  E  S  E  N  T
            M  T  A  E  V  I  G  H  E
            E  O  J  E  S  U  S
```

Word Bank (in bold letters)

"**Now** the **Feast** of **Unleavened Bread, called** the **Passover**, was **approaching**, and **the chief priests** and the **teachers** of the **law** were **looking** for **some way to** (10) get **rid** (2) of **Jesus**, for **they** were **afraid** of the **people**. Then **Satan entered Judas,** called **Iscariot,** one of the **Twelve**. And Judas **went** to the chief priests **and** the **officers of** (8) **the temple guard** and **discussed** with them how **he** (10) **might betray** Jesus. They were **delighted** and **agreed to give** him **money**. He **consented,** and **watched for an** (11) opportunity to **hand** (2) Jesus **over** to them **when no** (3) **crowd** was **present.** " Luke 22:1-6

All letters except fifteen X's should be circled.

Jesus Changes Water to Wine
John 2:1-11

Read the Scripture, then circle each word from the word bank hidden in the puzzle. Words may appear forward or backwards, moving up, down, or diagonally.

```
U  G  N  D  E  W  B  R  I  M  O  J  L  I  L  A  U
T  E  V  E  A  L  E  E  N  A  S  E  J  A  R  S  I
P  P  A  R  S  U  S  T  V  S  O  T  E  M  N  I  W
Q  N  E  B  H  K  T  A  I  T  T  H  W  S  V  G  Y
I  W  N  O  T  I  D  W  T  E  H  A  S  I  X  N  A
W  E  D  D  I  N  G  O  E  R  I  V  E  H  T  S  E
A  E  E  R  A  D  D  A  N  D  R  E  P  A  E  H  C
S  L  A  A  F  W  K  N  I  R  D  Y  H  W  U  Y  I
H  I  R  W  T  A  S  T  E  D  N  E  E  B  Q  E  O
E  L  P  I  C  S  I  D  O  S  E  R  V  A  N  T  H
T  A  D  E  N  R  U  T  E  N  O  T  S  A  A  C
U  G  E  T  A  M  O  O  R  G  E  D  I  R  B  S  R
O  O  M  I  N  G  L  H  O  L  D  I  N  G  O  I  E
R  N  R  M  A  U  S  P  E  O  J  E  R  O  M  D  V
E  E  O  E  C  E  G  L  R  R  E  A  L  I  Z  E  E
H  E  F  A  L  S  N  A  E  Y  S  E  O  F  W  A  A
T  N  R  D  L  T  I  C  H  O  U  M  S  I  O  C  L
O  I  E  A  I  S  R  E  T  U  S  O  L  L  N  H  E
M  W  P  Y  F  Y  B  R  A  E  N  C  A  L  L  E  D
```

Word Bank

THIRD	WEDDING	DAY	CANA	GALILEE	JESUS
MOTHER	DISCIPLE(S)	INVITE(D)	WINE	TIME	SERVANT(S)
SIX	STONE	JARS	JEWS	FILL (2)	WATER
BRIM	DRAW	MASTER	BANQUET	TASTED	TURNED
REALIZE	BRIDEGROOM	CHOICE	CHEAPER	GUESTS	DRINK
BEST	MIRACULOUS	SIGNS	PERFORMED	GLORY	FAITH
COME	GONE	OUT	YET	BEEN	WHY
WASH(ING)	NOW	ALSO	EACH	CALLED	THERE
MORE	ASIDE	REVEALED	HOLDING	BRINGS	AND
NOT	THE	NEARBY	PLACE	YOU	DO (9)
KIND	SO(9)	DEAR	HAVE	WAS	

SS2880

Jesus Clears the Temple
John 2:12-25

Read the Scripture, then circle each word from the word bank hidden in the puzzle. Words may appear forward or backwards, moving up, down, or diagonally.

```
H   M   E   L   A   S   U   R   E   J   S   O   L   D   B
E   O   O   D   E   N   R   U   T   R   E   V   O   R   W
X   N   D   R   A   H   S   T   A   Y   E   D   O   R   E
C   E   Y   O   O   S   S   C   R   I   P   T   U   R   E
H   Y   U   V   T   I   U   E   E   R   H   T   D   R   P
A   N   M   E   Y   W   H   I   P   E   F   A   E   A   S
N   M   O   T   H   E   R   T   R   H   E   R   S   S   U
G   U   S   H   D   J   S   D   R   O   C   S   T   C   O
I   A   U   T   H   O   R   I   T   Y   O   E   R   A   L
N   N   E   E   A   M   V   O   U   V   S   L   O   T   U
G   R   V   M   S   B   A   E   E   E   U   L   Y   T   C
S   E   O   P   I   N   L   R   S   T   S   I   Y   E   A
Y   P   R   L   O   A   M   E   K   A   E   N   D   R   R
A   A   P   E   P   E   E   H   S   E   J   G   O   E   I
D   C   A   T   T   L   E   R   K   E   T   T   B   D   M
```

Word Bank

CAPERNAUM	SELLING	OVERTURNED	MOTHER	CATTLE
MARKET	BROTHER(S)	SHEEP	SOLD	DOVES
PROVE	STAYED	TABLES	MIRACULOUS	DAYS
EXCHANGING	AUTHORITY	MONEY	DESTROY	SCATTERED
JEWISH	WHIP	PASSOVER	CORDS	THREE
JESUS	DROVE	BODY	JERUSALEM	SCRIPTURE
TEMPLE				

Bonus: To discover what Jesus said, write the uncircled letters on the lines below.

_____

_____

Jesus Teaches Nicodemus
John 3:1-21

Read the Scripture, then circle each word from the word bank hidden in the puzzle. Words may appear forward or backwards, moving up, down, or diagonally.

```
C  O  U  N  C  I  L  N  A  M  J  E  S  U  S
S  Y  S  P  I  R  I  T  D  N  I  W  O  X  K
W  U  M  H  E  A  V  E  N  O  T  A  R  D  A
O  D  N  A  T  S  R  E  D  N  U  T  A  O  E
L  U  S  R  N  K  B  U  T  E  X  E  E  G  P
B  E  L  I  E  V  E  D  E  E  T  R  H  K  S
I  B  N  S  V  Y  D  D  S  S  R  E  I  N  U
R  I  I  E  A  F  E  I  T  I  B  N  A  O  O
T  B  A  E  E  I  S  A  I  R  G  K  A  D  L
H  B  G  S  H  T  I  S  M  D  E  N  N  L  U
A  A  A  R  E  S  R  M  O  T  H  E  R  O  C
M  R  O  F  R  E  P  M  N  U  T  F  I  L  A
G  N  I  O  G  T  R  G  Y  A  N  R  O  B  R
J  E  W  I  S  H  U  L  L  E  T  D  I  N  I
H  T  U  R  T  H  S  E  L  F  S  E  S  O  M
```

Word Bank

PHARISEES	AGAIN	SOUND	JEWISH	MAN
KINGDOM	TELL	COUNCIL	OLD	HEAVEN (2)
JESUS	MOTHER(S)	UNDERSTAND	MOSES	RABBI
WATER	SPEAK	LIFT(ED)	SPIRIT	TESTIFY
GOD	FLESH	WIND	SEEN	PERFORM
BIRTH	SAID	SNAKE	MIRACULOUS	SURPRISED
TESTIMONY	SIGN(S)	TRUTH	BELIEVED	BORN
HEAR	ETERNAL	BUT	ONE (2)	BLOWS
ASK(ED)	ARE	NOT	GOING	

Bonus: To discover what Jesus told Nicodemus, write the uncircled letters on the lines below. (Two X's are not used.) _____

_____

Jesus Feeds Five Thousand
John 6:1-15

Read the Scripture, then circle each word from the word bank hidden in the puzzle. Words may appear forward or backwards, moving up, down, or diagonally.

```
E  V  I  F  S  D  W  O  R  C  O  S  W  D  D
S  U  A  T  W  E  R  D  N  A  S  A  E  I  N
U  N  S  M  A  L  L  X  A  A  S  S  N  S  A
S  E  W  P  D  A  H  P  R  E  S  U  O  T  R
E  A  T  B  J  E  I  G  I  O  R  P  U  R  E
J  M  L  C  F  O  G  O  R  C  B  B  G  I  H
T  S  E  T  A  W  A  C  T  E  S  O  H  B  T
E  I  T  F  I  T  J  E  R  S  V  I  Y  U  A
L  C  I  E  K  H  E  K  S  B  N  O  D  T  G
Y  K  B  L  B  O  Y  R  I  E  I  B  W  E  E
E  E  L  I  L  A  G  E  T  S  F  R  P  D  V
L  O  A  V  E  S  S  A  K  R  F  A  M  H  L
R  E  H  T  H  A  N  K  S  S  N  F  E  S  E
A  H  I  L  L  S  I  D  E  A  S  Y  J  I  W
B  D  E  W  O  L  L  O  F  T  S  A  E  F  T
```

Word Bank

JESUS	TEST	LEFT	FAR	CROSSED
SO (6)	SIT	SAT	GALILEE	BITE
GRASS	THE	CROWD	ANDREW	THANKS
BY	FOLLOWED	BOY (2)	DISTRIBUTED	TO (2)
UP(2)	FIVE	ENOUGH	HAD	SICK
SMALL	EAT (2)	LET	HILLSIDE	BARLEY
GATHER	AND	ON (2)	DISCIPLES	LOAVES
TWELVE	FEAST	TWO	ASK(ED)	OVER
FISH	BREAD	SAW		

Bonus: Shade in the uncircled letters to find out how many people Jesus fed. (One *X* is not used.)

SS2880

The Good Shepherd
John 10:1-21

Read the Scripture, then circle each word from the word bank hidden in the puzzle. Words may appear forward or backwards, moving up, down, or diagonally.

```
R  Y  A  W  G  N  I  H  T  O  N  A  M  H  C  T  A  W  G
E  E  J  E  S  U  S  O  S  V  E  R  S  E  N  K  M  X  O
C  T  B  S  E  Y  E  E  A  N  W  E  D  N  L  B  D  A  O
E  R  Y  B  V  N  D  A  V  I  P  U  K  T  U  Q  N  N  D
I  U  P  R  O  F  T  R  O  M  H  I  S  R  C  J  A  E  R
V  T  E  M  L  R  P  S  D  O  E  S  X  S  D  B  M  P  E
E  H  E  M  A  N  F  E  I  H  T  S  N  I  M  Z  M  R  C
D  D  H  N  A  M  E  F  O  R  R  E  E  L  M  N  O  E  O
A  E  S  L  A  E  T  S  A  E  T  M  T  S  E  D  C  H  G
L  E  R  A  I  O  A  N  T  S  U  L  U  D  H  L  L  T  N
L  D  E  I  V  F  G  N  I  U  L  S  R  P  D  G  I  A  I
J  E  W  S  H  E  E  L  P  N  A  R  T  S  I  N  M  F  Z
L  S  O  X  R  X  D  H  D  E  V  L  N  H  V  I  B  S  E
L  S  L  Y  A  W  O  M  I  S  P  O  O  E  I  V  S  R  X
I  E  F  Y  E  R  D  E  W  K  D  D  W  P  D  A  O  E  E
K  S  M  C  D  V  E  V  E  N  N  M  O  H  E  R  W  T  R
R  S  I  M  F  F  F  W  A  I  H  A  N  E  D  N  N  T  U
E  O  B  S  W  K  T  B  F  L  T  I  K  R  K  X  S  A  T
V  P  T  E  N  S  A  S  L  L  A  C  S  D  M  A  N  C  S
E  A  A  S  J  G  O  U  T  U  O  Y  D  I  A  S  T  S  A
N  W  O  L  L  O  F  L  A  E  T  S  S  B  L  I  N  D  P
```

Word Bank

TRUTH	JESUS	FOLLOW	RECOGNIZE	CALLS	FIND	SHEEP
STEAL (2)	STRANGER	PASTURE	COMMAND	GO (3)	GATE	KILL
SAVED	SCATTERS	RECEIVED	CLIMBS	MAN (3)	LIFE(2)	NAME
NOTHING	OF (2)	JEWS	THIEF	LOVES	FULL	IT (7)
DIVIDED	KNOW	ROBBER	WAY (2)	GOOD	FATHER	FOR (2)
DOES	DEMON	YOU	HIS (2)	EYES	BLIND	
SHEPHERD	VOICE	LAYS	PEN	POSSESSED	SEE	
WATCHMAN	HIRED	OWNS	RAVING	AM (7)	OPENS	
MY	MAD	OUT	LISTEN	SAID	ENTERS	
ABANDONS	NEVER	BY (2)	ALL	WOLF	TAKE	

Bonus: Shade in the uncircled letters to see one of the shepherd's tools. (Seven *X*'s are not used.)

Shining Star Publications, Copyright © 1993 SS2880

Jesus Raises Lazarus
John 11:38-44

Read the Scripture, then circle each word from the word bank hidden in the puzzle. Words may appear forward or backwards, moving up, down, or diagonally.

```
L  I  N  E  N  K  N  A  H  T  Y  S  A  I  D
L  L  E  M  Y  E  S  E  V  A  R  G  A  O  E
E  H  D  A  U  Z  M  U  K  O  O  T  G  T  P
T  I  M  C  L  O  T  H  R  E  L  P  O  E  P
D  E  L  L  A  C  Y  J  L  A  G  N  K  N  A
A  M  S  S  I  S  T  E  R  E  Z  A  B  E  R
R  A  D  R  D  T  N  S  E  N  T  A  E  E  W
T  R  N  G  U  T  V  U  H  E  R  E  L  B  U
I  T  A  O  R  O  E  S  T  A  N  D  I  N  G
F  H  H  A  I  M  F  Y  A  W  A  L  E  E  S
E  A  N  C  O  B  L  S  F  S  M  O  V  E  D
N  C  E  C  C  P  I  D  O  A  M  O  E  E  A
E  O  N  C  E  H  U  E  V  A  C  K  D  R  Y
B  E  O  E  N  O  T  S  D  R  A  E  H  O  S
B  A  D  U  L  S  A  W  D  E  A  D  T  M  R
```

Word Bank

JESUS	DEEPLY	MOVED	CAME	TOMB	CAVE	STONE
LAID	ENTRANCE	TAKE	AWAY	MARTHA	SISTER	DEAD
BAD	ODOR	FOUR	DAYS	BELIEVED	GLORY	GOD
LOOKED	FATHER	THANK	HEARD	BENEFIT	PEOPLE	YOU
SENT	CALLED	LOUD	VOICE	LAZARUS	HANDS	TELL
WRAPPED	LINEN	STANDING	CLOTH	FACE	GRAVE	HIS
COME	WAS	SAID	BEEN	THE	HERE	DID
NOT (2)	OUT	MAY	LET	ONCE	TOOK	ME (5)
MORE	SEE (2)	GO (3)				

Bonus: To discover what Jesus said to Lazarus, write the uncircled letters on the line below.

_____

SS2880

Jesus Washes His Disciples' Feet
John 13:1-17

Read the Scripture, then circle each word from the word bank hidden in the puzzle. Words may appear forward or backwards, moving up, down, or diagonally.

```
D I S C I P L E S P L O S N E
S Y W R L K D A A R E U I V X
I A R G O O Y R D O S S E C T
M R A N R O T L U E A N L B E
O T P I D T R H J B I E R L N
N E P N U O G O I N A D E E T
P B E R W A S H G N I N H S R
E R D U E N G R F T G A C S U
T E E T S A E F E M I T A E T
E T W E O V L O E E W S E D H
R S O R O W H I T A D R T A D
E A H S A A E S Z L L E A V E
W M S I N T A L H E M D V Y V
O A S D F E D D R Y I N G O I
P T S E E R E H T A F U T X L
```

Word Bank

PASSOVER	FEAST	JESUS	TIME	LEAVE	WORLD	FATHER
LOVED	SHOWED	EXTENT	EVENING	MEAL	DEVIL	JUDAS
BETRAY	POWER	RETURNING	TOOK	CLOTHING	TOWEL	TRUTH
WRAPPED	WAIST	WATER	BASIN	WASH	DISCIPLES	FEET
DRYING	SIMON PETER	REALIZE	UNDERSTAND	PART	HANDS	HEAD
CLEAN	TEACHER	LORD	MASTER	BLESSED		

Bonus: To discover what Peter asked Jesus, write the uncircled letters on the lines below. (One *X* is not used.)_____

_____

Saul's Conversion
Acts 9:1-19

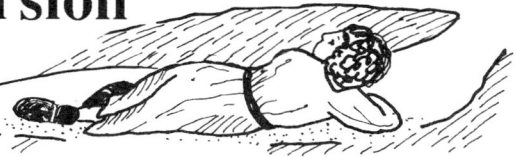

Read the Scripture, then circle each word from the word bank hidden in the puzzle. Words may appear forward or backwards, moving up, down, or diagonally.

```
L E L T D M Y M L Y D S H S S
I S O R R U S T U A I D A Y U
G U R O I R R N A W S N R N C
H O D P N D E E S A C A M A S
T H T E K E N M H G I H J G A
D A O R S R O U D O P I U O M
S G N L E O S R E T L S D G A
D N E A Y U I T L L E F A U D
E I V S E S R S L A S U S E J
Z H A R C E P N I N U H E S T
I T E E H M V I F A S K E D S
T A H T O W O H R N R K R O E
P E O T S N I T N I A S H O R
A R S E E E C L L A T A T F R
B B Y L N M E L A S U R E J A
```

Word Bank

SAUL	BREATHING	MURDEROUS	DISCIPLES	HIGH	ASKED
LETTERS	SYNAGOGUES	DAMASCUS	WAY	MEN	PRISONERS
ASK	ON (4)	JERUSALEM	HANDS	HE (8)	AS (12)
ALL	HOW	LIGHT	HEAVEN	FELL	VOICE
JESUS	GOT (2)	MY (2)	EYES	THREE	DAY(S)
FOOD	DRINK	HIS	ANANIAS	HOUSE	JUDAS
TARSUS	REPORT(S)	LORD	HARM	SAINT (S)	ARREST
INSTRUMENT	CHOSEN	SEE (5)	BY	BROTHER	ROAD
FILLED	HOLY SPIRIT	ME (3)	BAPTIZED		

Shining Star Publications, Copyright © 1993

SS2880

Paul and Silas in Prison
Acts 16:16-40

Read the Scripture, then circle each word from the word bank hidden in the puzzle. Words may appear forward or backwards, moving up, down or diagonally.

```
M E N C O U R A G E D S N S L
O S E I R D N D E N R A E W Y
N C I K S R A B A P T I Z E D
E O T L O O M E W R W H I J I
Y R H I A W O A A A D A T J A
S T P A R S R T S O E R I A E
R E T A L I M E H R Z M C I K
E D R A U U P N E P I C N L A
Y S V V T L M S D U E N M E U
A E E S A E L E R P S O Y R Q
R C N C A N L I T D D S H C H
P A E L K L T M I D N I G H T
D E P P I R T S O Y U R T A R
O P O F L R I G B E O P S I A
E V E I L E B A V E W J D N E
```

Word Bank

PLACE	PRAYER	GIRL	SLAVE	ENCOURAGED	EARNED	MONEY
PAUL	SERVANTS	SEIZED	SILAS	JEWS	UPROAR	ACCEPT
STRIPPED	BEATEN	PRISON	MIDNIGHT	HYMN(S)	JOY	SPIRIT
EARTHQUAKE	OPEN	CHAIN(S)	JAILER	WOKE	SWORD	KILL
HARM	BELIEVE	WASHED	WOUNDS	MEAL	BAPTIZED	FILLED
RELEASE	PEACE	ROMAN	CITIZEN(S)	ESCORTED	LYDIA(S)	

Bonus: To discover what the Philippian jailer asked, write the uncircled letters on the lines below.

_____

_____

Love
1 Corinthians 13:1-13

Read the Scripture, then circle each word from the word bank hidden in the puzzle. Words may appear forward or backwards, moving up, down, or diagonally.

```
A  C  P  E  E  K  S  U  R  M  G  A  F  S  D  T  L  B  I
Y  W  I  L  L  N  N  F  E  B  C  L  A  E  E  H  K  O  W
N  R  S  X  H  O  P  E  T  P  B  I  I  U  R  R  A  M  S
I  O  T  O  W  W  A  Y  S  Y  T  A  T  G  E  E  E  B  U
A  O  S  T  A  L  K  E  D  N  U  F  H  N  G  E  P  O  R
M  P  U  G  M  E  L  N  N  T  P  W  R  O  N  G  S  A  R
E  I  R  N  Y  D  A  V  A  M  O  U  N  T  A  I  N  S  E
R  F  T  O  S  G  B  Y  C  E  H  P  O  R  P  P  M  T  N
G  U  F  G  T  E  M  T  L  F  B  B  I  T  O  A  A  N  D
B  N  G  P  E  E  Y  R  A  S  O  E  T  S  I  T  N  X  E
E  K  I  L  R  L  C  U  N  E  D  H  C  E  K  I  N  D  R
S  X  F  K  I  O  X  T  G  R  Y  I  E  T  N  E  R  A  P
P  G  T  H  E  V  U  H  S  E  U  N  F  A  O  N  O  K  E
E  P  E  T  S  E  L  D  D  V  C  D  R  E  W  T  B  G  R
K  M  P  S  H  D  S  L  N  E  H  G  E  R  N  U  E  A  S
O  S  R  N  G  G  O  F  A  S  I  A  P  G  H  S  H  E  E
E  R  O  E  R  S  U  E  L  R  L  I  S  E  N  N  R  R  R
K  H  P  G  E  U  B  O  S  E  D  N  Y  W  P  N  D  G  V
V  I  H  N  D  L  A  G  H  P  S  M  U  R  T  K  C  H  E
Y  A  C  E  I  N  B  U  N  T  D  E  V  R  E  U  C  Y  S
A  F  E  T  R  D  N  M  B  C  E  V  M  N  S  R  S  U  T
```

Word Bank

SPEAK	KIND	PERSEVERES	TONGUES	ENVY	FAIL
LOVE	BOAST	GONG	PROUD	TALKED	CYMBAL
RUDE	PERFECTION	GIFT	SELF-SEEKING	THOUGHT	PROPHECY
ANGERED	WAYS	MYSTERIES	WRONGS	BEHIND	REMAIN
KNOWLEDGE	TRUTH	SURRENDER	FAITH	PROTECTS	TO (13)
MOUNTAINS	TRUST	PATIENT	HOPE	GREATEST	IS (6)
NOW	BODY	THREE	MAN	KNOWN	OF (3)
AM (4)	ARE	THE	POOR	ALL	IF (2)
CLANG(ING)	BUT	LIKE	CHILD	AND (4)	CAN
DOES	KEEP(S)	PUT	WILL	GAIN	

Bonus: Shade in the circled words to find a symbol of love. (Three *X's* are not used, but need to be colored.)

SS2880

Fruit of the Spirit
Galatians 5:13-26

Read the Scripture, then circle each word from the word bank hidden in the puzzle. Words may appear forward or backwards, moving up, down, or diagonally.

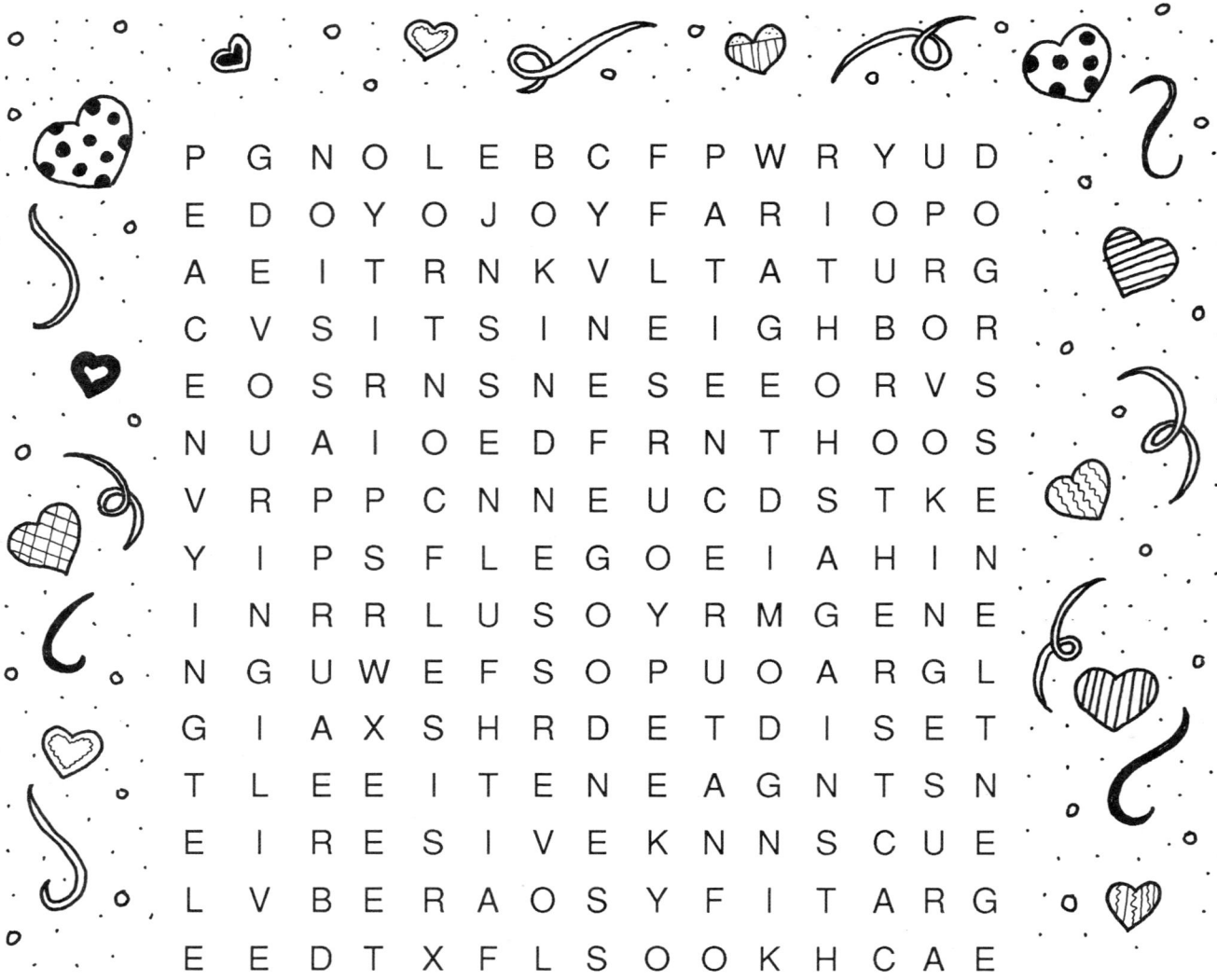

```
P G N O L E B C F P W R Y U D
E D O Y O J O Y F A R I O P O
A E I T R N K V L T A T U R G
C V S I T S I N E I G H B O R
E O S R N S N E S E E O R V S
N U A I O E D F R N T H O O S
V R P P C N N E U C D S T K E
Y I P S F L E G O E I A H I N
I N R R L U S O Y R M G E N E
N G U W E F S O P U O A R G L
G I A X S H R D E T D I S E T
T L E E I T E N E A G N T S N
E I R E S I V E K N N S C U E
L V B E R A O S Y F I T A R G
E E D T X F L S O O K H C A E
```

Word Bank

BROTHERS	KINGDOM	GOD	FREE	USE
FRUIT	BELONG	CONTRARY	ACTS	BE (3)
LOVE	SELF-CONTROL	JOY (2)	NATURE	SERVE
PEACE	PASSION	NEIGHBOR	PATIENCE	YOU
YOURSELF	KINDNESS	LIVE	GOODNESS	SPIRIT
DEVOURING	FAITHFULNESS	DESTROYED	GENTLENESS	RAGE
GRATIFY	PROVOKING	ENVY	AGAINST	OF (3)
ENVYING	LAW (2)	KEEP	LET (2)	EACH

Bonus: To discover what you need in your life, write the uncircled letters on the lines below. (Two *X* 's are not used.) _____

SS2880

Children and Parents

Ephesians 6:1-4

Read the Scripture, then circle each word from the word bank hidden in the puzzle. Words may appear forward or backwards, moving up, down, or diagonally.

```
G  C  O  M  M  A  N  D  M  E  N  T  E  X  A  S  P  E  R  A  T  E  T  H  E  S
O  G  N  I  N  I  A  R  T  O  D  I  N  E  R  D  L  I  H  C  Y  E  B  O  D  R
Q  E  B  R  M  N  C  D  J  V  M  N  M  D  M  N  M  E  G  H  C  I  H  W  L  E
R  I  Y  R  L  P  R  I  T  O  B  S  W  R  E  H  T  A  F  M  U  O  Y  I  D  H
P  N  O  E  K  A  X  N  S  F  K  T  V  H  T  R  A  E  C  D  I  G  L  U  A  T
S  D  U  H  W  R  P  G  Y  E  M  R  S  E  F  I  L  X  H  R  L  Q  Y  O  E  A
D  N  O  T  L  E  E  M  N  W  F  U  T  P  L  L  U  H  I  O  L  J  O  Y  T  F
V  A  G  O  M  N  R  T  O  N  U  C  J  G  N  I  R  B  L  L  E  P  J  T  S  H
T  Y  A  M  E  T  U  A  N  D  M  T  H  T  S  R  I  F  D  X  W  S  N  A  N  O
U  R  J  G  B  S  T  B  C  F  L  I  W  C  D  G  H  Y  R  A  U  N  E  H  I  N
R  I  G  H  T  W  E  L  L  P  R  O  M  I  S  E  I  A  E  P  N  W  I  T  H  O
M  O  T  H  E  R  R  U  O  Y  G  N  O  L  E  H  T  M  N  O  T  D  Y  O  U  R
```

Word Bank

CHILDREN (2)	OBEY	PARENTS	LORD	RIGHT	HONOR
FATHER	MOTHER (2)	FIRST	COMMANDMENT	ENJOY	LONG
LIFE	EARTH	EXASPERATE	INSTEAD	BRING	TRAINING
INSTRUCTION	YOUR (2)	WHICH	WELL (2)	MAY (2)	YOU (3)
DO (5)	NOT (3)	UP	WITH	IN (8)	THE (2)
IS (2)	FATHERS	THAT	IT (6)	GO (8)	AND (3)
OF	TO (6)	PROMISE			

Bonus: To discover how you should respond to your parents, shade in the uncircled areas. (Two *X*'s are not used.)

SS2880

Answer Key

THE BIRTH OF JESUS (Page 5)

Bonus: Star

THE BEATITUDES (Page 6)

Bonus: "B" (blessed)

PRAYER (Page 7)

Bonus: "This is how you should pray: 'Our Father in heaven, hallowed be your name . . . .'"

JESUS SENDS OUT THE TWELVE (Page 8)

Bonus: 12

JESUS WALKS ON THE WATER (Page 9)

Bonus: Jesus walks on the water.

THE TRANSFIGURATION (Page 10)

Bonus: "Don't be afraid." When they looked up, they saw no one except Jesus.

THE LORD'S SUPPER (Page 11)

Bonus: Chalice (goblet)

JESUS BEFORE PILATE (Page 12)

Bonus: "Which one do you want me to release to you, Barabbas or Jesus . . . .?"

Shining Star Publications, Copyright © 1993

SS2880

THE CRUCIFIXION (Page 13)

Bonus: Cross

THE DEATH OF JESUS (Page 14)

Bonus: My god, My God, why have you forsaken me?

THE BURIAL OF JESUS (Page 15)

Bonus: "Going to Pilate he asked for Jesus' body and Pilate ordered that it be given to him."

THE RESURRECTION (Page 16)

Bonus: "He is not here; He has risen."

THE GREAT COMMISSION (Page 17)

Bonus: Go

JAIRUS' DAUGHTER (Page 18)

Bonus: "Don't be afraid; just believe."

JESUS AND THE CHILDREN (Page 19)

Bonus: And He took the children in His arms, put His hands on them and blessed them.

BLIND BARTIMAEUS (Page 20)

Bonus: "Go, your faith has healed you."

THE TRIUMPHAL ENTRY (Page 21)

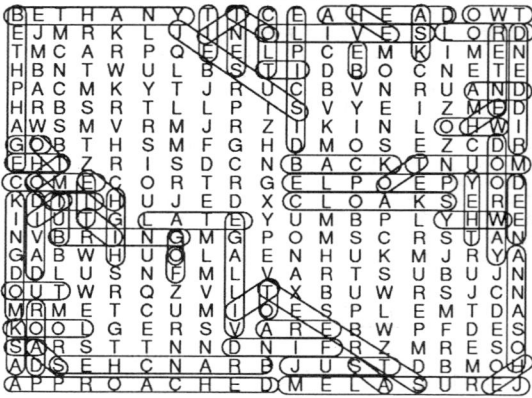

Bonus: Palm leaves design

THE GREATEST COMMANDMENT (Page 22)

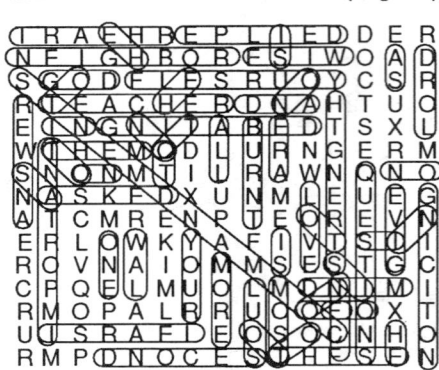

Bonus: Love

JESUS PREDICTS PETER'S DENIAL (Page 23)

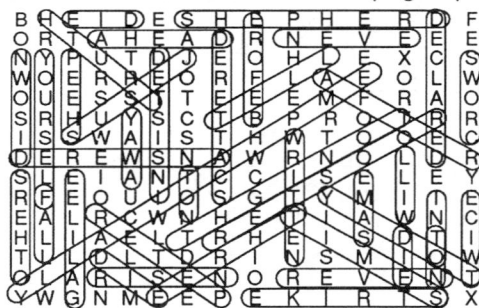

Bonus: "Before the rooster crows twice you. . .will disown me . . ."

GETHSEMANE (Page 24)

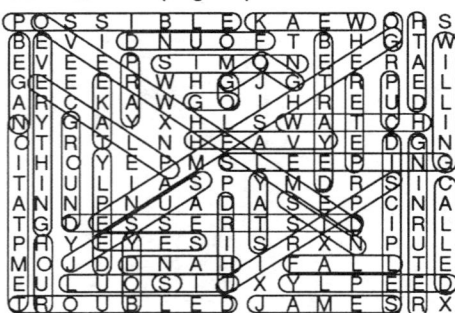

Bonus: "Sit here while I pray."

THE BIRTH OF JOHN THE BAPTIST (Page 25)

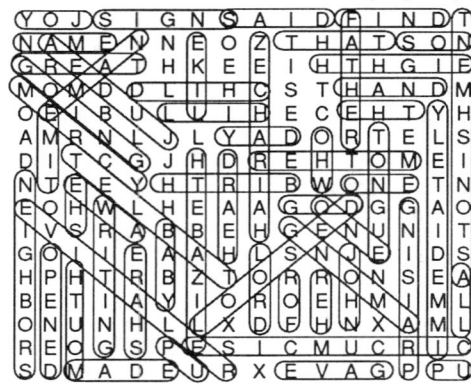

Bonus: "No! He is to be called John."

THE BOY JESUS AT THE TEMPLE (Page 26)

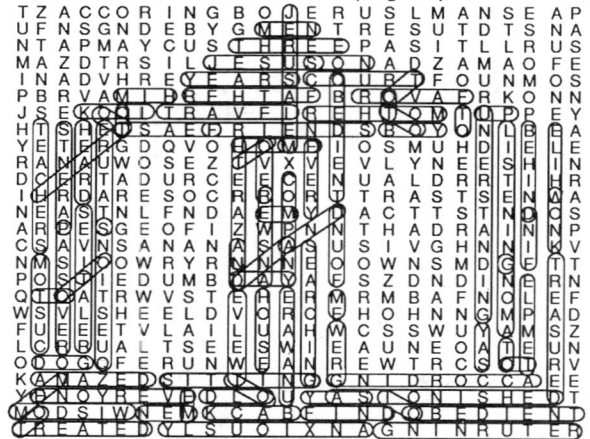

Bonus: Temple

THE TEMPTATION OF JESUS (Page 27)

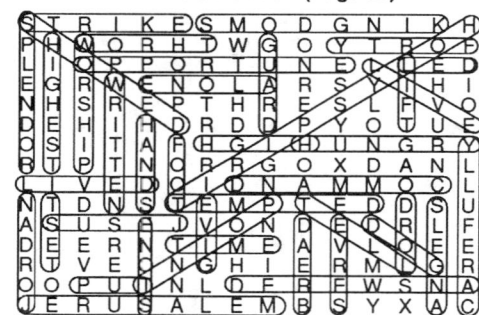

Bonus: "Worship the Lord Your God and serve him only."

JESUS CALMS THE STORM (Page 28)

Bonus: "Where is your faith?"

MARY AND MARTHA (Page 29)

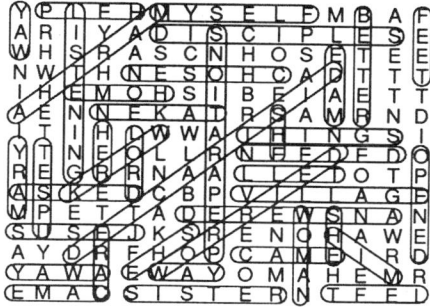

Bonus: "Mary has chosen what is better, and it will not be taken away from her."

ZACCHAEUS (Page 30)

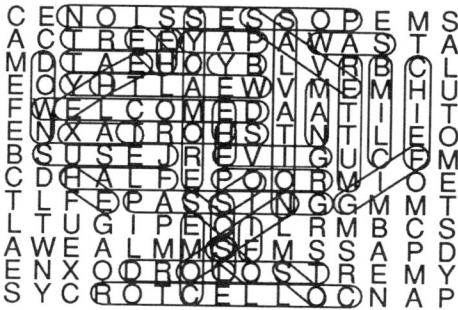

Bonus: Tree

JUDAS AGREES TO BETRAY JESUS (Page 31)

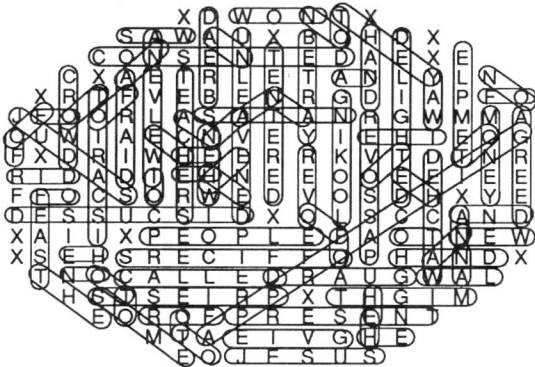

JESUS CHANGES WATER TO WINE (Page 32)

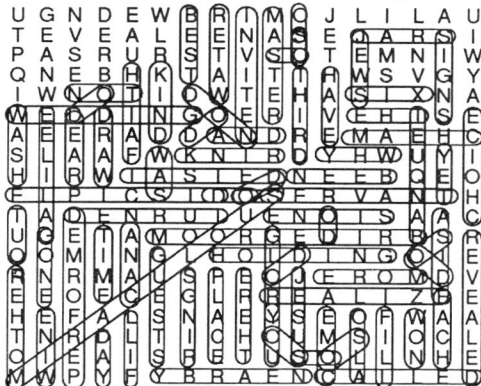

JESUS CLEARS THE TEMPLE (Page 33)

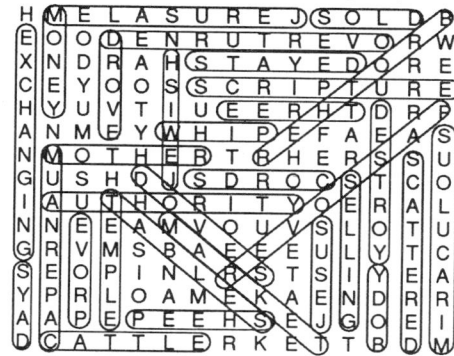

Bonus: "How dare you turn my Father's house into a market.."

JESUS TEACHES NICODEMUS (Page 34)

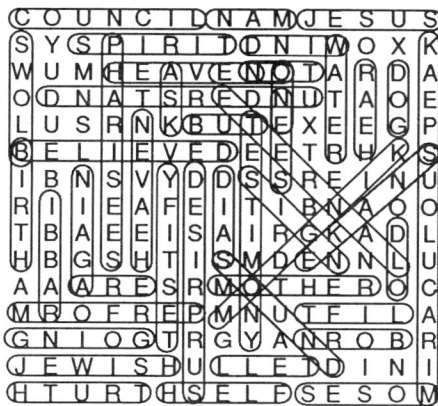

JESUS FEEDS FIVE THOUSAND (Page 35)

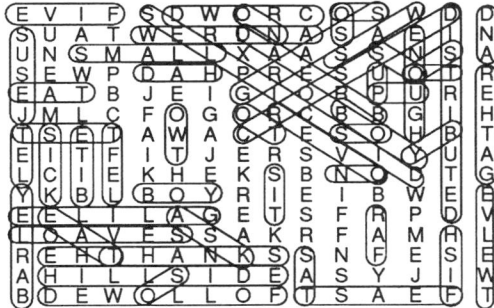

Bonus: 5000

THE GOOD SHEPHERD (Page 36)

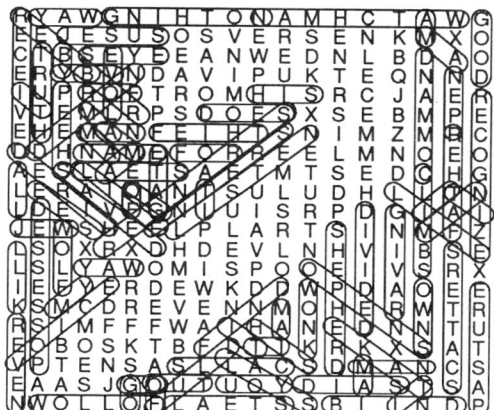

Bonus: Staff

JESUS RAISES LAZARUS (Page 37)

Bonus: "Lazarus, come out!"

JESUS WASHES HIS DISCIPLES' FEET (Page 38)

Bonus: "Lord, are you going to wash my feet?"

SAUL'S CONVERSION (Page 39)

PAUL AND SILAS IN PRISON (Page 40)

Bonus: "Sirs, what must I do to be saved?"

LOVE (Page 41)

Bonus: Heart

FRUIT OF THE SPIRIT (Page 42)

Bonus: Fruit of the Spirit

CHILDREN AND PARENTS (Page 43)

Bonus: Obey

SS2880